Becoming Your Own Therapist

New Expanded Edition

Including

Make Your Mind an Ocean

Previously published by the LAMA YESHE WISDOM ARCHIVE

Advice for Monks and Nuns, by Lama Yeshe and Lama Zopa Rinpoche
Virtue and Reality, by Lama Zopa Rinpoche
Teachings from the Vajrasattva Retreat, by Lama Zopa Rinpoche
Daily Purification: A Short Vajrasattva Practice, by Lama Zopa Rinpoche
The Essence of Tibetan Buddhism, by Lama Yeshe
Making Life Meaningful, by Lama Zopa Rinpoche
Teachings from the Mani Retreat, by Lama Zopa Rinpoche
Direct and Unmistaken Method, by Lama Zopa Rinpoche
The Yoga of Offering Food, by Lama Zopa Rinpoche

For initiates only:

A Chat about Heruka, by Lama Zopa Rinpoche
A Chat about Yamantaka, by Lama Zopa Rinpoche

In association with TDL Publications, Los Angeles:

Mirror of Wisdom, by Geshe Tsultim Gyeltsen
Illuminating the Path to Enlightenment, by His Holiness the Dalai Lama

May whoever sees, touches, reads, remembers, or talks or thinks about these books never be reborn in unfortunate circumstances, receive only rebirths in situations conducive to the perfect practice of Dharma, meet only perfectly qualified spiritual guides, quickly develop bodhicitta and immediately attain enlightenment for the sake of all sentient beings.

Lama Yeshe

Becoming Your Own Therapist
An Introduction to the Buddhist Way of Thought

New Expanded Edition
Including

Make Your Mind an Ocean
Aspects of Buddhist Psychology

Edited by Nicholas Ribush

LAMA YESHE WISDOM ARCHIVE • BOSTON

www.LamaYeshe.com

A non-profit charitable organization for the benefit of all
sentient beings and a section of the Foundation for the
Preservation of the Mahayana Tradition
www.fpmt.org

Becoming Your Own Therapist
First published for free distribution 1998
57,000 copies in print

Make Your Mind an Ocean
First published for free distribution 1999
37,000 copies in print

This combined edition first published 2003
15,000 copies for free distribution

LAMA YESHE WISDOM ARCHIVE
PO Box 356, Weston MA 02493
USA

ISBN 1-891868-13-6
10 9 8 7 6 5 4 3 2 1

Front cover photo Ricardo de Aratanha
Back cover photo Jacqueline Keeley
Book design by Mark Gatter and L.J.Sawlit

Please contact the LAMA YESHE WISDOM ARCHIVE
for more free copies of this book

CONTENTS

PUBLISHER'S ACKNOWLEDGMENTS

We are extremely grateful to our friends and supporters who have made it possible for the LAMA YESHE WISDOM ARCHIVE to both exist and function: to Lama Yeshe and Lama Zopa Rinpoche, whose kindness is impossible to repay; to Peter and Nicole Kedge and Venerable Ailsa Cameron for helping bring the ARCHIVE to its present state of development; to Venerable Roger Kunsang, Lama Zopa's tireless assistant, for his kindness and consideration; and to our sustaining supporters: Drs. Penny Noyce & Leo Liu, Barry & Connie Hershey, Joan Terry, Roger & Claire Ash-Wheeler, Claire Atkins, Doren & Mary Harper, Tom & Suzanne Castles, Hawk Furman, Richard Gere and Lily Chang Wu.

In particular, we would like to thank our long-time friend Thubten Yeshe, who has been such a great support to the LAMA YESHE WISDOM ARCHIVE since its inception, for her kind sponsorship of this book, a combined edition of Lama Yeshe's ever-popular *Becoming Your Own Therapist* and *Make Your Mind an Ocean,* which up to now have been published as separate books. Since those who have enjoyed one have invariably enjoyed the other, we decided to put them together into a single volume and, again, are extremely grateful to t.y. for making it possible.

We are also deeply grateful to those who have also been major contributors or book sponsors over the past few years: Dean Alper, Paula Antony, Christine Arlington, Peggy Bennington, Dharmawati Brechbuhl, Ross Brooke, Rose Canfield, the Caytons (Lori, Karuna, Pam, Bob & Amy), Lai-Hing Chong, Ngawang Chotak, Kok Leng Chuah, John Clulow, Denise Dagley, Paula de Wijs-Koolkin, Chris Dornan, Cecily Drucker, Derek & Soon Hui Goh, Dan & Tara Bennett Goleman, Lorraine Greenfield, Richard F. Hay, Heruka

Center, Wendy Hobbs, Su Hung, Ecie Hursthouse, Barbara Jenson, Kadampa Center, Bill Kelly & Robyn Brentano, Eric Klaft, Tony LaGreca, Land of Medicine Buddha, Chiu-Nan Lai, Chiu-Mei Lai, Henry & Catherine Lau, Salim Lee, Harry Leong (in loving memory of his father, Woon Leong), Mony & Ester Liberman, SS Lim, Judy Mindrol Lin, Jamieson Lowe, Sandra Magnussen, Doss McDavid, Kathleen McDonald, Ellen McInerney, Amy McKhann, Petra McWilliams, Tara Melwani, Therese Miller, Lynda Millspaugh, Ueli Minder, Janet Moore, Jack Morison, Esther Ngai, Trong Nguyen, Gerard O'Halloran, Dennis Paulson, James Pelkey, Leslie Reincke, Dorian Ribush, Rev. Janyce Riedel, Claire Ritter, Ven. Ingeborg Sandberg, Mayra Rocha Sandoval, Jesse Sartain, Jack Sonnabaum & Judith Hunt, Datuk Tai Tsu Kuang, Tan Swee Eng, Tom Thorning, Thubten Norbu Ling Center, Tushita Retreat Centre, Wendy van den Heuvel, Diana van Die (in loving memory of Lenie van Die), Oanh Vovan, Tom Waggoner & Renee Robison, Vajrapani Institute, Robbie Watkins and Wisdom Publications.

We would like, as well, to express our appreciation for the kindness and compassion of all those other generous benefactors mentioned in detail in our previous publications and those who have contributed funds to our work since our last published list a couple of years ago. They are too numerous to mention individually in this book, but we value highly each and every donation made to spreading the Dharma for the sake of the kind mother sentient beings and now pay tribute to you all on our Web site, www.LamaYeshe.com. Thank you so much.

I would also like to pay tribute to our dear and long-time friend and supporter who helped us and many other Dharma and Tibet-related projects for almost thirty years, Carol Davies, who passed way in Perth earlier this year, far too soon. May she and all other sentient beings immediately realize bodhicitta and quickly attain supreme enlightenment.

I also thank the many kind people who have asked that their donations be kept anonymous; the volunteers who have given so generously of their time to help us with our mailings, especially

Therese Miller; my wife, Wendy Cook, for her tireless help and support; our dedicated office staff, Jennifer Barlow and Linda Merle; Alison Ribush & Mandala Books (Melbourne) and Veronica Kaczmarowski & FPMT Australia for much appreciated assistance with our work in Australia; and Dennis Heslop, Philip Bradley and our other friends at Wisdom Books (London) for their great help with our work in Europe. We appreciate, too, the kindness and expertise of our main volunteer transcribers, Su Hung, Segen Speer-Senner and Gareth Robinson. We also thank most sincerely Massimo Corona and the FPMT International Office for their generous financial and administrative assistance.

Finally, I want to express my gratitude to Greg Sneddon and his wonderful team of volunteers in Melbourne, Australia—including Dr. Su Hung, Anne Pottage, Llysse Valez, Chris Friedl and Anthony Deague—who recently completed digitizing almost our entire archive of more than 10,000 hours of teachings by Lama Yeshe and Lama Zopa Rinpoche and will continue to help us in this area.

Special gratitude is extended to Mark Gatter for his excellent design of the original versions of this book, which has been beautifully adapted by L.J.Sawlit in the development of this combined edition.

If you, dear reader, would like to join this noble group of openhearted altruists by contributing to the production of more free books by Lama Yeshe or Lama Zopa Rinpoche or to any other aspect of the LAMA YESHE WISDOM ARCHIVE's work, please contact us to find out how.

— *Dr. Nicholas Ribush*

Through the merit of having contributed to the spread of the Buddha's teachings for the sake of all sentient beings, may our benefactors and their families and friends have long and healthy lives, all happiness, and may all their Dharma wishes be instantly fulfilled.

Part One

Becoming Your Own Therapist
An Introduction to the Buddhist Way of Thought

EDITOR'S INTRODUCTION

Lama Yeshe's teachings are unique. Nobody taught like Lama. Spontaneous, from the heart, in the moment, direct; every word an instruction to be practiced. Lama's English was unique. Nobody spoke like Lama. Highly creative, Lama expressed himself not only verbally, but physically and facially as well. How to convey this miracu-lous transmission on paper? As I have noted elsewhere, those of us presented with this challenge do the best we can.

As Lama frequently liked to point out, his teachings were not dry, academic, philosophical discourses but practical, down-to-earth methods for looking within and understanding the mind. Lama always challenged us to find out who we are, what we are. In his inimitable, provocative style, he would dare us to examine our pre-conceptions fearlessly, in the hope that we would see for ourselves how everything comes from the mind; that we create our own suf-fering and happiness; that we must take personal responsibility for whatever we experience, good or bad.

In this section we offer three talks by Lama Yeshe on the general topic of Buddhism. They were public lectures given almost thirty years ago to mainly Western audiences. Nevertheless, as Lama also liked to point out, Lord Buddha's timeless teachings are as univer-sally relevant today as they were when they were first given, over 2,500 years ago. Therefore, there is no doubt that now, a mere three decades down the road, Lama Yeshe's teachings are as globally appli-cable as they were back in the seventies.

Each lecture is followed by a question and answer session. Lama and his audiences always enjoyed the give and take of these lively exchanges, and pretty much anything went. For most people, it was their first ever encounter with a Tibetan lama, and they brought along several years' worth of questions. As is apparent, Lama handled everything with great compassion, humor and aplomb.

Although these talks were called lectures, I think Lama would have each of us use them as a mirror for our mind and look beyond the words, find ourselves, and become our own psychologist.

I would like to thank Cheryl Bentsen, Rand Engel and Wendy Cook for their insightful comments, which greatly improved the edited version of these talks.

FINDING OURSELVES THROUGH BUDDHISM

When we study Buddhism, we are studying ourselves, the nature of our own minds. Instead of focusing on some supreme being, Buddhism emphasizes more practical matters, such as how to lead our lives, how to integrate our minds and how to keep our everyday lives peaceful and healthy. In other words, Buddhism always accentuates experiential knowledge-wisdom rather than some dogmatic view. In fact, we don't even consider Buddhism to be a religion in the usual sense of the term. From the lamas' point of view, Buddhist teachings are more in the realm of philosophy, science or psychology.

The human mind instinctively seeks happiness. East, West—there's no difference; everybody's doing the same thing. But if your search for happiness causes you to grasp emotionally at the sense world, it can be very dangerous. You have no control.

Now, don't think that control is an Eastern thing, a Buddhist thing. We all need control, especially those of us caught up in the materialistic life; psychologically, emotionally, we're too involved in objects of attachment. From the Buddhist point of view, that's an unhealthy mind; you're mentally ill.

Actually, you already know that external, scientific technological development alone cannot satisfy the desires of your attachment or solve your other emotional problems. But what Lord Buddha's teaching shows you is the characteristic nature of human potential, the capacity of the human mind. When you study Buddhism, you learn what you are and how to develop further; instead of emphasizing some kind of supernatural belief system, Buddhist methods teach you to develop a deep understanding of yourself and all other phenomena.

However, whether you are religious or a materialist, a believer or an atheist, it is crucial that you know how your own mind works. If you don't, you'll go around thinking you're healthy, when in reality, the deep root of afflictive emotions, the true cause of all psychological disease, is there, growing within you. Because of that, all it takes is some tiny external thing changing, something insignificant going wrong, and within a few seconds, you're completely upset. To me, that shows you're mentally ill. Why? Because you're obsessed with the sense world, blinded by attachment, and under the control of the fundamental cause of all problems—ignorance of the true nature of your own mind.

It doesn't matter if you try to refute what I'm saying by telling me that you don't believe it. It's not a question of belief. No matter how much you say, "I don't believe I have a nose," your nose is still there, right between your eyes. Your nose is always there, whether you believe it or not.

I've met many people who proudly proclaim, "I'm not a believer." They're so proud of their professed lack of belief in anything. You check up; this is important to know. In the world today there are so many contradictions. Scientific materialists boast, "I don't believe"; religious people say, "I believe." But no matter what you think, you still need to know the characteristic nature of your own mind. If you don't, then no matter how much you talk about the shortcomings of attachment, you have no idea what attachment actually is or how to control it. Words are easy. What's really difficult is to understand the true nature of attachment.

For example, when people first made cars and planes, their intention was to be able to do things more quickly so that they'd have more time for rest. But what's happened instead is that people are more restless than ever. Examine your own everyday life. Because of attachment, you get emotionally involved in a concrete sense world of your own creation, denying yourself the space or time to see the reality of your own mind. To me, that's the very definition of a difficult life. You cannot find satisfaction or enjoyment. The truth is that pleasure and joy actually come from the mind, not from external phenomena.

Nevertheless, some intelligent, skeptical people do understand to a degree that material objects do not guarantee a worthwhile, enjoyable life and are trying to see if there really is something else that might offer true satisfaction.

When Lord Buddha spoke about suffering, he wasn't referring simply to superficial problems like illness and injury, but to the fact that the dissatisfied nature of the mind itself is suffering. No matter how much of something you get, it never satisfies your desire for better or more. This unceasing desire is suffering; its nature is emotional frustration.

Buddhist psychology describes six basic emotions that frustrate the human mind, disturbing its peace, making it restless: ignorance, attachment, anger, pride, deluded doubt and distorted views. These are mental attitudes, not external phenomena. Buddhism emphasizes that to overcome these delusions, the root of all suffering, belief and faith are not much help: you have to understand their nature.

If you do not investigate your own mind with introspective knowledge-wisdom, you will never see what's in there. Without checking, no matter how much you talk about your mind and your emotions, you'll never really understand that your basic emotion is egocentricity and that this is what's making you restless.

Now, to overcome your ego you don't have to give up all your possessions. Keep your possessions; they're not what's making your life difficult. You're restless because you are clinging to your possessions with attachment. Ego and attachment pollute your mind, making it unclear, ignorant and agitated and preventing the light of wisdom from growing. The solution to this problem is meditation.

Meditation does not imply only the development of single-pointed concentration, sitting in some corner doing nothing. Meditation is an alert state of mind, the opposite of sluggishness; meditation is wisdom. You should remain aware every moment of your daily life, fully conscious of what you are doing and why and how you are doing it.

We do almost everything unconsciously. We eat unconsciously; we drink unconsciously; we talk unconsciously. Although we claim conscious, we are completely unaware of the afflictions rampaging through our minds, influencing everything we do.

Check up for yourselves; experiment. I'm not being judgmental or putting you down. This is how Buddhism works. It gives you ideas that you can check out in your own experience to see if they're true or not. It's very down-to-earth; I'm not talking about something way up there in the sky. It's actually a very simple thing.

If you don't know the characteristic nature of attachment and its objects, how can you generate loving kindness towards your friends, your parents or your country? From the Buddhist point of view, it's impossible. When you hurt your parents or your friends, it's your unconscious mind at work. When acting out his anger, the angry person is completely oblivious as to what's happening in his mind. Being unconscious makes us hurt and disrespect other sentient beings; being unaware of our own behavior and mental attitude makes us lose our humanity. That's all. It's so simple, isn't it?

These days, people study and train to become psychologists. Lord Buddha's idea is that everybody should become a psychologist. Each of you should know your own mind; you should become your own psychologist. This is definitely possible; every human being has the ability to understand his or her own mind. When you understand your own mind, control follows naturally.

As I said, don't think that control is just some Himalayan trip or that it must be easier for people who don't have many possessions. That's not necessarily true. Next time you are emotionally upset, check for yourself. Instead of distracting yourself by busily doing something, relax and try to become aware of what you're doing. Ask yourself, "Why am I doing this? How am I doing it? What's the cause?" You will find this to be a wonderful experience. Your main problem is a lack of intensive knowledge-wisdom, awareness, or consciousness. Therefore, you will discover that through understanding, you can easily solve your problems.

To feel loving kindness for others, you have to know the nature of the object. If you don't, then even though you say, "I love him; I love her," it's just your arrogant mind taking you on yet another ego trip. Make sure you know how and why. It is very important that you become your own psychologist. Then you can treat yourself through the understanding wisdom of your own mind; you'll be able to relax with and enjoy your friends and possessions instead of becoming restless and berserk and wasting your life.

To become your own psychologist, you don't have to learn some big philosophy. All you have to do is examine your own mind every day. You already examine material things every day—every morning you check out the food in your kitchen—but you never investigate your mind. Checking your mind is much more important.

Nevertheless, most people seem to believe the opposite. They seem to think that they can simply buy the solution to whatever problem they're facing. The materialistic attitude that money can buy whatever you need to be happy, that you can purchase a peaceful mind, is obviously not true, but even though you may not say the words, this is what you're thinking. It's a complete misconception.

Even people who consider themselves religious need to understand their own minds. Faith alone never stops problems; understanding knowledge-wisdom always does. Lord Buddha himself said that belief in Buddha was dangerous; that instead of just believing in something, people should use their minds to try to discover their own true nature. Belief based on understanding is fine—once you realize or are intellectually clear about something, belief follows automatically—but if your faith is based on misconceptions, it can easily be destroyed by what others say.

Unfortunately, even though they consider themselves religious, many spiritually inclined people are weak. Why? Because they don't understand the true nature of their minds. If you really know what your mind is and how it works, you'll understand that what's preventing you from being healthy is only mental energy. When you understand your own mind's view, or perception, of the world, you'll realize that not only are you constantly grasping at the sense world, but also that what you're grasping at is merely imaginary. You will see that you're too concerned with what's going to happen in a non-existent future and totally unconscious of the present moment, that you are living for a mere projection. Don't you agree that a mind that is unconscious in the present and constantly grasping at the future is unhealthy?

It is important to be conscious in your everyday life. The nature of conscious awareness and wisdom is peace and joy. You don't need to grasp at some future resultant joy. As long as you follow the path of right understanding and right action to the best of your ability, the result will be immediate, simultaneous with the action. You don't have to think, "If I spend my lifetime acting right, perhaps I'll get some good result in my next life." You don't need to obsess over the attainment of future realizations. As long as you act in the present with as much understanding as you possibly can, you'll realize everlasting peace in no time at all.

And I think that's enough from me. Better that we have a question and answer session, instead of my talking all the time. Thank you.

Q: When you were talking about meditation, you didn't mention visualization. It seems that some people find it relatively easy to visualize while others find it quite difficult. How important is it to develop the ability to visualize things in the mind?
Lama: Many people have trouble visualizing what's described to them simply because they have not trained their minds in it, but for others it's because they have a poor imagination; they're too physical. Perhaps they think that all there is to their being is their physical body; that there's no mind apart from their brain. However, Buddhism has methods whereby you can train your mind and develop the ability to visualize in meditation. But in reality, you visualize all day long. The breakfast you eat in the morning is a visualization. Whenever you go shopping and think, "This is nice," or "I don't like that," whatever you're looking at is a projection of your own mind. When you get up in the morning and see the sun shining and think, "Oh, it's going to be nice today," that's your own mind visualizing. Actually, visualization is quite well understood. Even shopkeepers and advertising agents know the importance of visualization, so they create displays or

billboards to attract your attention: "Buy this!" They know that things you see affect your mind, your visualization. Visualization is not something supernatural; it's scientific.

Q: From what you say, I get the impression you're somewhat critical of the West, that you laugh at what we do and the way we try to civilize the uncivilized. I don't really have a question, but what future do you see for mankind in terms of what the so-called progressive West is developing: bigger planes, bigger houses, bigger supermarkets? What future do you see for the West?

Lama: I see that Western people are getting busier and busier, more and more restless. I'm not criticizing material or technological development as such, but rather the uncontrolled mind. Because you don't know who or what you are, you spend your life blindly grasping at what I call "supermarket goodness." You agitate your own life; you make yourself restless. Instead of integrating your life, you splinter it. Check up for yourself. I'm not putting you down. In fact, Buddhism doesn't allow us to dogmatically put down anybody else's way of life. All I'm trying to suggest is that you consider looking at things another way.

Q: Lama, like yourself, most of the Tibetan teachers we see are men. I was wondering if there are any female *rinpoches* or *tulkus?*

Lama: Yes, of course. Men and women are completely equal when it comes to developing higher states of mind. In Tibet, monks would sometimes take teachings from female rinpoches. Buddhism teaches that you can't judge people from the outside; you can't say, "He's nothing; I'm special." You can never really tell from outer appearances who's higher and who's lower.

Q: Is the role of a Buddhist nun very different from that of a monk?

Lama: Not really. They study the same things and teach their students in the same way.

Q: Sometimes it's hard to find a teacher. Is it dangerous to try to practice tantra, for example, without a teacher, just by reading books?

Lama: Yes, very dangerous. Without specific instructions, you can't just pick up a book on tantra and think, "Wow, what fantastic ideas. I want to practice this right now!" That kind of attitude never brings realizations. You need the guidance of an experienced teacher. Sure, the ideas are fantastic, but if you don't know the method, you can't put them into your own experience; you have to have the key. Many Buddhist books have been translated into English. They'll tell you, "Attachment is bad; don't get angry," but how do you actually abandon attachment and anger? The Bible, too, recommends universal love, but how do you bring universal love into your own experience? You need the key, and sometimes only a teacher can give you that.

Q: What should people in the West do when they can't find a teacher? Should those who are really searching go to the East to find one?

Lama: Don't worry. When the time is right, you'll meet your teacher. Buddhism doesn't believe that you can push other people: "Everybody should learn to meditate; everybody should become a Buddhist." That's stupid. Pushing people is unwise. When you're ready, some kind of magnetic energy will bring you together with your teacher. About going to the East, it depends on your personal situation. Check up. The important thing is to search with wisdom and not blind faith. Sometimes, even if you go to the East, you still can't find a teacher. It takes time.

Q: What is the Buddhist attitude towards suicide?

Lama: People who take their own lives have no understanding of the purpose or value of being born human. They kill themselves out of ignorance. They can't find satisfaction, so they think, "I'm hopeless."

Q: If a person, out of ignorance perhaps, believes he has achieved enlightenment, what is his purpose in continuing to live?

Lama: An ignorant person who thinks he's enlightened is completely mentally polluted and is simply compounding the ignorance he already has. All he has to do is to check the actions of his uncontrolled mind and he'll realize he's not enlightened. Also, you don't have to ask others, "Am I enlightened?" Just check your own experiences. Enlightenment is a highly personal thing.

Q: I like the way that you stress the importance of understanding over belief, but I find it difficult to know how a person brought up in the West or given a scientific education can understand the concept of reincarnation: past, present and future lives. How can you prove that they exist?

Lama: If you can realize your own mind's continuity from the time you were a tiny embryo in your mother's womb up to the present time, then you'll understand. The continuity of your mental energy is a bit like the flow of electricity from a generator through the wires until it lights up a lamp. From the moment it's conceived, as your body evolves, mental energy is constantly running through it— changing, changing, changing—and if you can realize that, you can more easily understand your own mind's *previous* continuity. As I keep saying, it's never simply a question of *belief.* Of course, initially it's difficult to accept the idea of reincarnation because these days it's such a new concept for most people, especially those brought up in the West. They don't teach you continuity of consciousness in school; you don't study the nature of the mind—who you are, what you are—in college. So of course, it's all new to you. But if you think it's important to know who and what you are, and you investigate your mind through meditation, you will easily come to understand the difference between your body and your mind; you will recognize the continuity of your own consciousness; from there you will be able to realize your previous lives. It is not necessary to accept reincarnation on faith alone.

Q: Could you please explain the relationship between meditation, enlightenment and supernormal mental powers, such as seeing the future, reading other people's minds and seeing what's happening in a place that's far away?

Lama: While it's definitely possible to achieve clairvoyance through developing single-pointed concentration, we have a long way to go. As you slowly, slowly gain a better understanding of your own mind, you will gradually develop the ability to see such things. But it's not that easy, where you meditate just once and all of a sudden you can see the future or become enlightened. It takes time.

Q: If you are meditating, working towards enlightenment, do these powers come with control or just all of a sudden, with no control at all?
Lama: True powers come with control. They're not like the uncontrolled emotional hallucinations you experience after you've taken drugs. Even before you reach enlightenment, you can develop insight into your past and future lives and read other people's minds, but this comes about only through the controlled and gradual development of wisdom.

Q: Do you yourself have the power to separate your mind from your body and astral travel or do other things?
Lama: No.

Q: Does His Holiness the Dalai Lama have the power to do that?
Lama: The Mahayana Buddhism of Tibet certainly does contain an unbroken oral tradition of teachings on the development of supernormal powers, which has passed from realized guru to disciple from the time of the Buddha himself down to the present, but just because that teaching exists it doesn't mean that I have accomplished it. Furthermore, Tibetan Buddhism prohibits any lama who does have such realizations from proclaiming them. Even when you do attain enlightenment, unless there's a good reason, you're not allowed to go around telling everyone that you're a buddha. Be careful. Our system is different from yours. In the West, you hear of people who say, "Last night God spoke to me in my dreams." We think it can be dangerous for people to broadcast details of their mystical experiences, therefore, we don't allow it.

Q: Some years ago I read a book called *The Third Eye* about a gentleman who had extraordinary powers. Have many people had their third eye opened?

Lama: What the author of that book, Lobsang Rampa, says is a literal misconception. The third eye is not a physical thing but rather a metaphor for wisdom. Your third eye is the one that sees beyond ordinary sense perception into the nature of your own mind.

Q: Since Buddhism believes in reincarnation, can you tell me how long there is between lives?

Lama: It can be anything from a few moments up to seven weeks. The moment the consciousness separates from the body, the subtle body of the intermediate state is already there, waiting for it. Due to the force of craving for another physical body, the intermediate state being searches for an appropriate form, and when it finds one, it takes rebirth.

Q: How does Buddhism explain the population explosion? If you believe in reincarnation, how is it that the population is expanding all the time?

Lama: That's simple. Like modern science, Buddhism talks about the existence of billions and billions of galaxies. The consciousness of a person born on earth may have come from a galaxy far away, drawn here by the force of karma, which connects that person's mental energy to this planet. On the other hand, the consciousness of a person dying on this earth may at the time of death be karmically directed to a rebirth in another galaxy, far from here. If more minds are being drawn to earth, the population increases; if fewer, it declines. That does not mean that brand new minds are coming into existence. Each mind taking rebirth here on earth has come from its previous life—perhaps in another galaxy, perhaps on earth itself, but not from nowhere—in accordance with the cyclic nature of worldly existence.

Q: Is Buddhist meditation better than any other form of meditation or is it simply a case of different forms of meditation suiting different people?

Lama: I can't say that Buddhist meditation is better than that of other religions. It all depends upon the individual.

Q: If someone were already practicing one form of meditation, say, transcendental meditation, would there be any point in that person trying Buddhist meditation as well?

Lama: Not necessarily. If you find that your meditation practice completely awakens your mind and brings you everlasting peace and satisfaction, why try anything else? But if, despite your practice, your mind remains polluted and your actions are still uncontrolled—constantly, instinctively giving harm to others—I think you have a long way to go, baby. It's a very personal thing.

Q: Can a bodhisattva be a Marxist in order to create social harmony? I mean, is there a place for the bodhisattva in Marxism or, *vice versa,* is there a place in Marxism for the bodhisattva? Could Marxism be a tool in the abolition of all sentient beings' suffering?

Lama: Well, it's pretty hard for someone like me to comment on a bodhisattva's actions, but I doubt that a bodhisattva would become a communist in order to stop social problems. Problems exist in the minds of individuals. *You* have to solve your *own* problems, no matter what kind of society you live in—socialist, communist or capitalist. You must check your own mind. Your problem is not society's problem, not my problem. You are responsible for your own problems just as you're responsible for your own liberation or enlightenment. Otherwise you're going to say, "Supermarkets help people because they can buy the stuff they need in them. If I work in a supermarket I'll really be contributing to society." Then, after doing that for a while, you're going to say, "Maybe supermarkets don't help that much after all. I'd be of more help to others if I took a job in an office." None of those things solve social problems. But first of all you have to check where you got the idea that by becoming a communist, a bodhisattva could help all mother sentient beings.

Q: I was thinking that many people in the world today are hungry and deprived of basic needs and that while they're preoccupied with hunger and the safety and security of their families, it's hard for them to grasp the more subtle aspects of phenomena, such as the nature of their own minds.

Lama: Yes, I understand what you are saying. But don't forget that the starving person preoccupied by hunger and the obese person obsessing over what else to buy in the supermarket are basically the same. Don't just focus on those who are materially deprived. Mentally, rich and poor are equally disturbed, and, fundamentally, one is as unhappy as the other.

Q: But Lord Krishna united India in a spiritual war, the war of Dharma, and as a result, at one time, all the people of India had the ability to engage in spiritual practice. Couldn't we now spread the Dharma among all the people on earth and establish a better global society through a kind of spiritual socialism?

Lama: First of all, I think that what you're saying is potentially very dangerous. Only a few people would understand what you're talking about. Generally, you can't say that actions that give harm to mother sentient beings are those of a bodhisattva. Buddhism forbids you to kill other sentient beings, even for supposedly religious reasons. In Buddhism, there's no such thing as a holy war. You have to understand this. And secondly, it's impossible to equalize everybody on earth through force. Until you fully understand the minds of all beings throughout the universe and have abandoned the minds of self-cherishing and attachment, you will never make all living beings one. It's impossible.

Q: I don't mean making all people the same, because obviously there are going to be different mental levels. But we could establish a universal human society on the basis of socialistic economic theory.

Lama: I think you shouldn't worry about that. You'd be better off worrying about the society of your own mind. That's more worthwhile, more realistic than making projections about what's happening in the world around you.

Q: But is it not a spiritual practice to strike a balance between your own self-realization and service to humanity?

Lama: Yes, you can serve society, but you can't homogenize all sentient beings' actions simultaneously, just like that. Lord Buddha wants all sentient beings to become enlightened right away, but our negative karma is too strong, so we remain uncontrolled. You can't wave a magic wand, "I want everybody to be equally happy," and expect it to happen just like that. Be wise. Only a wise mind can offer equality and peace. You can't do it through emotional rationalization. And you have to know that communist ideas about how best to equalize sentient beings are very different from those of Lord Buddha. You can't mix such different ideas. Don't fantasize; be realistic.

Q: In conclusion, then, are you saying that it's impossible to create one common spiritual society on this planet?

Lama: Even if you could, it would not stop people's problems. Even if you made a single society of all the inhabitants of the entire universe, there would still be attachment, there would still be anger, there would still be hunger. Problems lie within each individual. People are not the same; everybody is different. Each of us needs different methods according to our individual psychological makeup, mental attitudes and personality; each of us needs a different approach in order to attain enlightenment. That's why Buddhism completely accepts the existence of other religions and philosophies. We recognize that they are all necessary for human development. You can't say that any one way of thinking is right for everybody. That's just dogma.

Q: What do you say about drugs that expand the consciousness? Can one experience the *bardo* under the influence of drugs?

Lama: Yes, it's possible—take an overdose and soon enough you'll experience the bardo. No, I'm just joking. There's no way to get the bardo experience through taking drugs.

Q: Can you read people's auras?

Lama: No, but everybody does have an aura. Aura means vibration. Each of us has our own mental and physical vibration. When you are psychologically upset, your physical environment changes visibly. Everybody goes through that. As science and Buddhism both assert, all physical matter has its own vibration. So people's mental states affect that vibration of their body, and these changes are reflected in the person's aura. That's the simple explanation of the aura. To gain a deep understanding, you have to understand your mind. First learn to read your own mind, then you'll be able to read the minds of others.

Q: How does meditation remove emotional blockages?
Lama: There are many different ways. One is through understanding the nature of your emotions. That way, your emotion is digested into knowledge-wisdom. Digesting your emotions by wisdom is really worthwhile.

Thank you. Good night. Thank you so much.

Auckland, New Zealand
7 June 1975

RELIGION: THE PATH OF INQUIRY

People have many different ideas about the nature of religion in general and Buddhism in particular. Those who consider religion and Buddhism at only the superficial, intellectual level will never understand the true significance of either. And those whose view of religion is even more superficial than that will not even consider Buddhism to be a religion at all.

First of all, in Buddhism we're not that interested in talking about the Buddha himself. Nor was he; he wasn't interested in people believing in him, so to this day Buddhism has never encouraged its followers simply to believe in the Buddha. We have always been more interested in understanding human psychology, the nature of the mind. Thus, Buddhist practitioners always try to understand their own mental attitudes, concepts, perceptions and consciousness. Those are the things that really matter.

Otherwise, if you forget about yourself and your delusions and focus instead on some lofty idea—like "What is Buddha?"—your spiritual journey becomes a dream-like hallucination. That's possible; be careful. In your mind there's no connection between Buddha, or God, and yourself. They're completely separate things: you're completely down here; Buddha, or God, is completely up there. There's no connection whatsoever. It's not realistic to think that way. It's too extreme. You're putting one thing down at the lower extreme and the other way up at the upper. In Buddhism, we call that kind of mind dualistic.

Furthermore, if humans are completely negative by nature, what is the point of seeking a higher idea? Anyway, ideas are not realizations. People always want to know all about the highest attainments or the nature of God, but such intellectual knowledge has nothing to do with their lives or their minds. True religion should be the pursuit of self-realization, not an exercise in the accumulation of facts.

In Buddhism, we are not particularly interested in the quest for intellectual knowledge alone. We are much more interested in understanding what's happening here and now, in comprehending our present experiences, what we are at this very moment, our fundamental nature. We want to know how to find satisfaction, how to find happiness and joy instead of depression and misery, how to overcome the feeling that our nature is totally negative.

Lord Buddha himself taught that basically, human nature is pure, egoless, just as the sky is by nature clear, not cloudy. Clouds come and go, but the blue sky is always there; clouds don't alter the fundamental nature of the sky. Similarly, the human mind is fundamentally pure, not one with the ego. Anyway, whether you are a religious person or not, if you can't separate yourself from your ego, you're completely misguided; you've created for yourself a totally unrealistic philosophy of life that has nothing whatsoever to do with reality.

Instead of grasping at intellectual knowledge, wanting to know what's the highest thing going, you'd be much better off trying to gain an understanding of the basic nature of your own mind and how to deal with it right now. It is so important to know how to act effectively: method is the key to any religion, the most important thing to learn.

Say you hear about an amazing treasure house containing jewels for the taking but don't have the key to the door: all your fantasies about how you'll spend your new-found wealth are a complete hallucination. Similarly, fantasizing about wonderful religious ideas and peak experiences but having no interest in immediate action or the methods of attainment is totally unrealistic. If you have no method, no key, no way to bring your religion into your everyday life, you'd be better off with Coca-Cola. At least that quenches your thirst. If your religion is simply an idea, it's as insubstantial as air. You should be very careful that you understand exactly what religion is and how it should be practiced.

Lord Buddha himself said, "Belief is not important. Don't believe what I say just because I said it." These were his dying words. "I have taught many different methods because there are many different individuals. Before you embrace any of them, use your wisdom to check that they fit your psychological make-up, your own mind. If my methods seem to make sense and work for you, by all means adopt them. But if you don't relate to them, even though they might sound wonderful, leave them be. They were taught for somebody else."

These days, you can't tell most people that they should believe something just because Buddha said, because God said. It's not enough for them. They'll reject it; they want proof. But those who cannot understand that the nature of their mind is pure will be unable to see the possibility of discovering their innate purity and will lose whatever chance they had to do so. If you think that your mind is fundamentally negative, you tend to lose all hope.

Of course, the human mind has both positive and negative sides. But the negative is transient, very temporary. Your up and down emotions are like clouds in the sky; beyond them, the real, basic human nature is clear and pure.

Many people misunderstand Buddhism. Even some professors of Buddhist studies look at just the words and interpret what the Buddha taught very literally. They don't understand his methods, which are the real essence of his teachings. In my opinion, the most important aspect of any religion is its methods: how to put that religion into your own experience. The better you understand how to do that, the more effective your religion becomes. Your practice becomes so natural, so realistic; you easily come to understand your own nature, your own mind, and you don't get surprised by whatever you find in it. Then, when you understand the nature of your own mind, you'll be able to control it naturally; you won't have to push so hard; understanding naturally brings control.

Many people will imagine that control of the mind is some kind of tight, restrictive bondage. Actually, control is a natural state. But you're not going to say that, are you? You're going to say that the mind is uncontrolled by nature, that it is natural for the mind to be uncontrolled. But it's not. When you realize the nature of your uncontrolled mind, control comes as naturally as your present uncontrolled state arises. Moreover, the only way to gain control over your mind is to understand its nature. You can never force your mind, your internal world, to change. Nor can you purify your mind by punishing yourself physically, by beating your body. That's totally impossible. Impurity, sin, negativity or whatever else you want to call it is psychological, a mental phenomenon, so you can't stop it physically. Purification requires a skillful combination of method and wisdom.

To purify your mind, you don't have to believe in something special up there—God, or Buddha. Don't worry about that. When you truly realize the up and down nature of your everyday life, the characteristic nature of your own mental attitude, you'll automatically want to implement a solution.

These days, many people are disillusioned with religion; they seem to think it doesn't work. Religion works. It offers fantastic solutions to all your problems. The problem is that people don't understand the characteristic nature of religion, so they don't have the will to implement its methods.

Consider the materialistic life. It's a state of complete agitation and conflict. You can never fix things to be the way you want. You can't just wake up in the morning and decide exactly how you want your day to unfold. Forget about weeks, months, or years; you can't even predetermine one day. If I were to ask you right now if you could get up in the morning and set exactly how your day was going to go, how you were going to feel each moment, what would you say? There's no way you could do that, is there?

No matter how much you make yourself materially comfortable, no matter how you arrange your house—you have this, you have that; you put one thing here, you put another there—you can never manipulate your mind in the same way. You can never determine the way you're going to feel all day. How can you fix your mind like that? How can you say, "Today I'm going to be like this"? I can tell you with absolute certainty, as long as your mind is uncontrolled, agitated and dualistic, there's no way; it's impossible. When I say this, I'm not putting you down; I'm just talking about the way the mind works.

What all this goes to show is that no matter how you make yourself materially comfortable, no matter how much you tell yourself, "Oh, this makes me happy, today I'm going to be happy all day long," it's impossible to predetermine your life like that. Automatically, your feelings keep changing, changing, changing. This shows that the materialistic life doesn't work. However, I don't mean that you should renounce the worldly life and become ascetics. That's not what I'm saying. My point is that if you understand spiritual principles correctly and act accordingly, you will find much greater satisfaction and meaning in your life than you will by relying on the sense world alone. The sense world alone cannot satisfy the human mind.

Thus, the only purpose for the existence of what we call religion is for us to understand the nature of our own psyche, our own mind, our own feelings. Whatever name we give to our spiritual path, the most important thing is that we get to know our own experiences, our own feelings. Therefore, the lamas' experience of Buddhism is that instead of emphasizing belief, it places prime importance on personal experimentation, putting Dharma methods into action and assessing the effect they have on our minds: do these methods help? Have our minds changed or are they just as uncontrolled as they ever were? This is Buddhism, and this method of checking the mind is called meditation.

It's an individual thing; you can't generalize. It all comes down to personal understanding, personal experience. If your path is not providing solutions to your problems, answers to your questions, satisfaction to your mind, you must check up. Perhaps there's something wrong with your point of view, your understanding. You can't necessarily conclude that there's something wrong with your religion just because you tried it and it didn't work. Different individuals have their own ideas, views, and understanding of religion, and can make mistakes. Therefore, make sure that the way you understand your religion's ideas and methods is correct. If you make the right effort on the basis of right understanding, you will experience deep inner satisfaction. Thus, you'll prove to yourself that satisfaction does not depend on anything external. True satisfaction comes from the mind.

We often feel miserable and our world seems upside-down because we believe that external things will work exactly as we plan and expect them to. We expect things that are changeable by nature not to change, impermanent things to last forever. Then, when they do change, we get upset. Getting upset when something in your house breaks shows that you didn't really understand its impermanent nature. When it's time for something to break, it's going to break, no matter what you expect.

Nevertheless, we still expect material things to last. Nothing material lasts; it's impossible. Therefore, to find lasting satisfaction, you should put more effort into your spiritual practice and meditation than into manipulating the world around you. Lasting satisfaction comes from your mind, from within you. Your main problem is your uncontrolled, dissatisfied mind, whose nature is suffering.

Knowing this, when any problem arises, instead of getting upset because of your unfulfilled expectations and busily distracting yourself with some external activity, relax, sit down and examine the situation with your own mind. That is a much more constructive way of dealing with problems and pacifying your mind. Moreover, when you do this, you allow your innate knowledge-wisdom to grow. Wisdom can never grow in an agitated, confused and restless mind.

Agitated mental states are a major obstacle to your gaining of wisdom. So too is the misconception that your ego and your mind's nature are one and the same. If that's what you believe, you'll never be able to separate them and reach beyond ego. As long as you believe that you are totally in the nature of sin and negativity you will never be able to transcend them. What you believe is very important and very effectively perpetuates your wrong views. In the

West, people seem to think that if you aren't one with your ego, you can't have a life, get a job or do anything. That's a dangerous delusion—you can't separate ego from mind, ego from life. That's your big problem. You think that if you lose your ego you'll lose your personality, your mind, your human nature.

That's simply not true; you shouldn't worry about that. If you lose your ego you'll be happy—you *should* be happy. But of course, this raises the question, what is the ego? In the West, people seem to have so many words for the ego, but do they know what the ego really is? Anyway, it doesn't matter how perfect your English is, the ego is not a word; the word is just a symbol. The actual ego is within you: it's the wrong conception that your self is independent, permanent and inherently existent. In reality, what you believe to be "I" doesn't exist.

If I were to ask everybody here to check deeply, beyond words, what they thought the ego was, each person would have a different idea. I'm not joking; this is my experience. You should check your own. We always say, very superficially, "That's your ego," but we have no idea what the ego really is. Sometimes we even use the term pejoratively: "Oh, don't worry, that's just your ego," or something like that, but if you check up more deeply, you'll see that the average person thinks that the ego is his personality, his life. Men feel that if they were to lose their ego, they'd lose their personalities, they'd no longer be men; women feel that were they to lose their ego they'd lose their female qualities. That's not true; not true at all. Still, based on Westerners' interpretation of life and ego, that's pretty much what it comes down to. They think the ego is something positive in the sense that it's essential for living in society; that if you don't have an ego, you can't mix in society. You check up more deeply—on the mental level, not the physical. It's interesting.

Even many psychologists describe the ego so superficially that you'd think it was a physical entity. From the Buddhist point of view, the ego is a mental concept, not a physical thing. Of course, symptoms of ego activity can manifest externally, such as when, for example, someone's angry and his face and body reflect that angry vibration. But that's not anger itself; it's a symptom of anger. Similarly, ego is not its external manifestations but a mental factor, a psychological attitude. You can't see it from the outside.

When you meditate, you can see why today you're up, tomorrow you're down: mood swings are caused by your mind. People who don't check within themselves come up with very superficial reasons like, "I'm unhappy today because the sun's not shining," but most of the time your ups and downs are due to primarily psychological factors.

When a strong wind blows, the clouds vanish and blue sky appears. Similarly, when the powerful wisdom that understands the nature of the mind arises, the dark clouds of ego disappear. Beyond the ego—the agitated, uncontrolled mind—lie everlasting peace and satisfaction. That's why Lord Buddha prescribed penetrative analysis of both your positive and your negative sides. In particular, when your negative mind arises, instead of being afraid, you should examine it more closely.

You see, Buddhism is not at all a tactful religion, always trying to avoid giving offense. Buddhism addresses precisely what you are and what your mind is doing in the here and now. That's what makes it so interesting. You can't expect to hear only positive things. Sure you have a positive side, but what about the negative aspects of your nature? To gain an equal understanding of both, an understanding of the totality of your being, you have to look at your negative characteristics as well as the positive ones, and not try to cover them up.

I don't have much more to say right now, but I'd be happy to try to answer some questions.

Q: Lama, were you saying that we should express rather than suppress our negative actions, that we should let the negativity come out?

Lama: It depends. There are two things. If the negative emotion has already bubbled to the surface, it's probably better to express it in some way, but it's preferable if you can deal with it before it has reached that level. Of course, if you don't have a method of dealing with strong negative emotions and you try to bottle them up deep inside, eventually that can lead to serious problems, such as an explosion of anger that causes someone to pick up a gun and shoot people. What Buddhism teaches is a method of examining that emotion with wisdom and digesting it through meditation, which allows the emotion to simply dissolve. Expressing strong negative emotions externally leaves a tremendously deep impression on your consciousness. This kind of imprint makes it easier for you to react in the same harmful way again, except that the second time it may be even more powerful than the first. This sets up a karmic chain of cause and effect that perpetuates such negative behavior. Therefore, you have to exercise skill and judgment in dealing with negative energy, learn when and how to express it and, especially, know how to recognize it early in the piece and digest it with wisdom.

Q: Could you please explain the relationship between Buddhist meditation techniques and hatha yoga?
Lama: In Buddhism we tend to focus more on penetrative intro-spection than on bodily movement, although there are certain prac-tices where the meditation techniques are enhanced by physical exercises. In general, Buddhist meditation teaches us to look within at what we are, to understand our own true nature. All the same, Buddhist meditation does not necessarily imply sitting in the lotus position with your eyes closed—meditation can be brought into every aspect of your daily life. It is important to be aware of every-thing you do so that you don't unconsciously harm either yourself or others. Whether you are walking, talking, working, eating…whatever you do, be conscious of the actions of your body, speech and mind.

Q: Do Buddhists control their *prana* [wind energy] completely through the mind?
Lama: Yes. If you can control your mind, you can control anything. It's impossible to control your physical body without first control-ling your mind. If you try to control your body forcibly, if you

pump yourself up with no understanding of the mind-body rela-tionship, it can be very dangerous and cause your mind great harm.

Q: Can you reach as deep a state of meditation through walking as you can through sitting?
Lama: Sure, it's theoretically possible, but it depends upon the individual. For beginners, it is obviously much easier to attain deeper states of concentration through sitting meditation. Experienced meditators, however, can maintain single-pointed concentration, a fully integrated mind, whatever they're doing, including walking. Of course, if someone's mind is completely dis-turbed, even sitting medi-tation may not be enough for him to integrate his mind. One of the hallmarks of Buddhism is that you can't say that everybody should do this, everybody should be like that; it depends on the individual. However, we do have a clearly defined, step-like path of meditation practice: first you develop this, then you move on to that, and so on through the various lev-els of concentration. Similarly, the entire path to enlightenment—we call it the *lam-rim*—has been laid out in a graded, logical fash-ion so that each person can find his or her own level and take it from there.

Q: Lama, can the various negative thoughts that arise in our minds come from a source outside of ourselves, from other people, or per-haps from spirits?
Lama: Well, that's a very good question. The real source, the deep root of negativity, lies within our own minds, but for this to mani-fest usually requires interaction with a cooperative, environmental cause, such as other people or the material world. For example, some people experience mood swings as a result of astrological influences, such as the vibration of planetary movement. Others' emotions fluctuate because of hormonal changes in their bodies. Such experiences do not come from their minds alone but through the interaction of physical and mental energy. Of course, we would also say that the fact that we find ourselves in a body susceptible to

this kind of change originally comes from our minds. But I don't think Lord Buddha would say that there is some outer spirit harming you like that. What is possible is that your inner energy is relating to some outer energy, and that it is that interaction that makes you sick.

You can see from your own life experiences how the environment can affect you. When you're among peaceful, generous, happy people, you're inclined to feel happy and peaceful yourself. When you're among angry, aggressive people, you tend to become like them. The human mind is like a mirror. A mirror does not discriminate but simply reflects whatever's before it, no matter whether it's horrible or wonderful. Similarly, your mind takes on the aspect of your surroundings, and if you're not aware of what's going on, your mind can fill with garbage. Therefore, it is very important to be conscious of your surroundings and how they affect your mind.

The thing that you have to understand about religion is how your religion relates to your own mind, how it relates to the life you lead. If you can manage that, religion is fantastic; the realizations are there. You don't need to emphasize belief in God, or Buddha, or sin or whatever; don't worry about all that. Just act out of right understanding as best you can and you'll get results, even today. Forget about super consciousness or super universal love—universal love grows slowly, steadily, gradually. If, however, you're just clinging to the notion, "Oh, fantastic! Infinite knowledge, infinite power," you're simply on a power trip. Of course, spiritual power really does exist, but the only way you can get it is by engaging in the proper spiritual actions. Power comes from within you; part of you becomes power, too. Don't think that the only true power is up there, somewhere in the sky. You have power; your mind is power.

Q: Perception is one of the five aggregates that, according to Buddhist philosophy, constitute a person. How does it work?
Lama: Yes, that's another good question. Most of the time, our perception is illusory; we're not perceiving reality. Sure, we see the sense world—attractive shapes, beautiful colors, nice tastes and so forth—

but we don't actually perceive the real, true nature of the shapes, colors and tastes we see. That's how most of the time our perception is mistaken. So our mistaken perception processes the information supplied by our five senses and transmits incorrect information to our mind, which reacts under the influence of the ego. The result of all this is that most of the time we are hallucinating, not seeing the true nature of things, not understanding the reality of even the sense world.

Q: Does past karma affect our perception?

Lama: Yes, of course. Past karma affects our perception a lot. Our ego grasps at our uncontrolled perception's view, and our mind just follows along: that entire uncontrolled situation is what we call karma. Karma is not simply some irrelevant theory; it's the everyday perceptions in which we live, that's all.

Q: Lama, what is the relationship between the body and mind as far as food is concerned.

Lama: Body is not mind, mind is not body, but the two have a very special connection. They are very closely linked, very sensitive to changes in each other. For example, when people take drugs, the substance doesn't affect the mind directly. But since the mind is connected to the body's nervous system and sense organs, changes induced in the nervous system by the drug throw it out of harmony and cause the mind to hallucinate. There's a very strong connection between the body and the mind. In Tibetan tantric yoga, we take advantage of that strong connection: by concentrating strongly on the body's psychic channels we can affect the mind accordingly. Therefore, even in everyday life, the food you eat and the other things your body touches have an effect on your mind.

Q: Is fasting good for you?

Lama: Fasting is not all that important unless you are engaged in certain special mind training practices. Then, fasting may even be essential. This is certainly the lamas' experience. For example, if you eat and drink all day and then try to meditate in the evening, your concentration will be very poor. Therefore, when we're doing serious meditation, we eat only once a day. In the morning, we just drink tea; at midday we have lunch; and in the evening, instead of eating, we again drink tea. For us, this kind of routine makes life desirably simple and the body very comfortable; but for someone not engaged in mind training, it would probably feel like torture. Normally, we don't advocate fasting. We tell people not to punish themselves but simply to be happy and reasonable and to keep their bodies as healthy as they can. If your body gets weak, your mind becomes useless. When your mind becomes useless, your precious human life becomes useless. But on special occasions, when fasting enhances your meditation practice, when there's a higher purpose, I would say yes, fasting can be good for you.

Thank you very much. If there are no further questions, I won't keep you any longer. Thank you very much.

Brisbane, Australia
28 April 1975

A GLIMPSE OF BUDDHIST PSYCHOLOGY

The study of Buddhism is not a dry, intellectual undertaking or the skeptical analysis of some religious, philosophical doctrine. On the contrary, when you study Dharma and learn how to meditate, *you* are the main topic; you are mainly interested in your own mind, your own true nature.

Buddhism is a method for controlling the undisciplined mind in order to lead it from suffering to happiness. At the moment, we all have undisciplined minds, but if we can develop a correct understanding of its characteristic nature, control will follow naturally and we'll be able to release emotional ignorance and the suffering it brings automatically. Therefore, no matter whether you are a believer or a non-believer, religious or not religious, a Christian, a Hindu, or a scientist, black or white, an Easterner or a Westerner, the most important thing to know is your own mind and how it works.

If you don't know your own mind, your misconceptions will prevent you from seeing reality. Even though you might say you're a practitioner of this religion or that, if you investigate more deeply, you might find that you are nowhere. Be careful. No religion is against your knowing your own nature, but all too frequently religious people involve themselves too much in their religion's history, philosophy or doctrine and ignore how and what they themselves are, their present state of being. Instead of using their religion to attain its goals—salvation, liberation, inner freedom, eternal happiness and joy—they play intellectual games with their religion, as if it were a material possession.

Without understanding how your inner nature evolves, how can you possibly discover eternal happiness? Where is eternal happiness? It's not in the sky or in the jungle; you won't find it in the air or under the ground. Everlasting happiness is within you, within your psyche, your consciousness, your mind. That's why it is so important that you investigate the nature of your own mind.

If the religious theory that you learn does not serve to bring happiness and joy into your everyday life, what's the point? Even though you say, "I'm a practitioner of this or that religion," check what you've done, how you've acted, and what you've discovered since you've been following it. And don't be afraid to question yourself in detail. Your own experience is good. It is essential to question everything you do, otherwise, how do you know what you're doing? As I'm sure you know already, blind faith in any religion can never solve your problems.

Many people are lackadaisical about their spiritual practice. "It's easy. I go to church every week. That's enough for me." That's not the answer. What's the purpose of your religion? Are you getting the answers you need or is your practice simply a joke? You have to check. I'm not putting anybody down, but you have to be sure of what you're doing. Is your practice perverted, polluted by hallucination, or is it realistic? If your path teaches you to act and exert yourself correctly and leads to spiritual realizations such as love, compassion and wisdom, then obviously it's worthwhile. Otherwise, you're just wasting your time.

The mental pollution of misconceptions is far more dangerous than drugs. Wrong ideas and faulty practice get deeply rooted in your mind, build up during your life, and accompany your mind into the next one. That is much more dangerous than some physical substance.

All of us, the religious and the non-religious, Easterner and Westerner alike, want to be happy. Everybody seeks happiness, but are you looking in the right place? Perhaps happiness is *here* but you're looking *there*. Make sure you seek happiness where it can be found.

We consider Lord Buddha's teaching to be more akin to psychology and philosophy than to what you might usually imagine religion to be. Many people seem to think that religion is mostly a question of belief, but if your religious practice relies mainly on faith, sometimes one skeptical question from a friend—"What on earth are you doing?"—can shatter it completely: "Oh my god! Everything I've been doing is wrong." Therefore, before you commit yourself to any spiritual path, make sure you know exactly what you're doing.

Buddhist psychology teaches that emotional attachment to the sense world results from physical and mental feelings. Your five senses provide information to your mind, producing various feelings, all of which can be classified into three groups: pleasant, unpleasant and neutral. These feelings arise in response to either physical or mental stimuli.

When we experience pleasant feelings, emotional attachment ensues, and when that pleasant feeling subsides, craving arises, the desire to experience it again. The nature of this mind is dissatisfaction; it disturbs our mental peace because its nature is agitation. When we experience unpleasant feelings, we automatically dislike and want to get rid of them; aversion arises, again disturbing our mental peace. When we feel neutral, we ignore what's going on and don't want to see reality. Thus, whatever feelings arise in our daily lives—pleasant, unpleasant or neutral—they disturb us emotionally and there's no balance or equanimity in our minds.

So, examining your own feelings in this way has nothing to do with belief, has it? This is not some Eastern, Himalayan mountain thing. This is you; this is your thing. You can't refute what I'm saying by claiming, "I have no feelings." It's so simple, isn't it?

Furthermore, many of our negative actions are reactions to feeling. See for yourself. When you feel pleasant as a result of contact with people or other sense objects, analyze exactly how you feel, why you feel pleasant. The pleasant feeling is not in the external object, is it? It's in your mind. I'm sure we can all agree that the pleasant feeling is not outside of you. So, why do you feel that way? If you experiment like this, you will discover that happiness and joy, discomfort and unhappiness, and neutral feelings are all within you. You will find that you yourself are mainly responsible for the feelings you experience and that you cannot blame others for the way you feel: "He makes me miserable; she makes me miserable; that stuff makes me miserable." You cannot blame society for your problems, although that's what we always do, isn't it? It's not realistic.

Once you realize the true evolution of your mental problems, you'll never blame any other living being for how you feel. That realization is the beginning of good communication with and respect for others. Normally, we're unconscious; we act unconsciously and automatically disrespect and hurt others. We don't care; we just do it, that's all.

Many people, even some psychologists, seem to think that you can stop the emotion of craving-desire by feeding it with some object or other: if you're suffering because your husband or wife has left you, getting another one will solve your problem. That's impossible. Without understanding the characteristic nature of your feelings of pleasant, unpleasant and neutral, you will never discover the nature of your mental attitudes, and without discovering that, you can never put an end to your emotional problems.

For instance, Buddhism says you should feel compassion and love for all living beings. How can you possibly feel even equanimity for all beings while the ignorant, dualistic mind is functioning so strongly within you? You can't, because emotionally you are too extreme. When you feel happy because a pleasant feeling has arisen through contact with a particular object, you grossly exaggerate what you consider to be the good qualities of that object, inflating your emotions as much as you possibly can. But you know that your mind can't stay up like that. It's impermanent, transitory, so of course, you soon crash back down. Then, automatically, your unbalanced mind gets depressed. You have to understand exactly how much energy you expend in pursuit of or in flight from mental feelings. We are always too extreme; we have to find the middle way.

If you look a little deeper, you will also find that feelings are responsible for all the conflict in the world. From two small children fighting over a piece of candy to two huge nations fighting over their very existence, what are they fighting for? For pleasant feelings. Even children too young to speak will fight because they want to feel happy.

Through meditation you can easily see the truth of all this. Meditation reveals everything that's in your mind; all your garbage, all your positivity; everything can be seen through meditation. But don't think that meditation means just sitting on the floor in the lotus position doing nothing. Being conscious, aware of everything that you do—walking, eating, drinking, talking—is meditation. The sooner you realize this, the quicker will you realize that you yourself are responsible for your actions, that you yourself are responsible for the happy feelings you want and the unhappy feelings you don't, and that nobody else controls you.

When a pleasant feeling arises and then, as is its nature, subsides, causing you to feel frustrated because you want it again, that's not created by God, Krishna, Buddha or any other outside entity. Your own actions are responsible. Isn't that easy to see? The weak mind thinks, "Oh, he made me sick, she makes me feel horrible." That's the weak mind at work, always trying to blame somebody or something else. Actually, I think that examining your everyday life experiences to see how your physical and mental feelings arise is a wonderful thing to do. You're learning all the time; there's no time that you're not learning. In that way, through the application of your own knowledge-wisdom, you will discover that the realization of everlasting peace and joy is within you. Unfortunately, the weak mind doesn't possess much knowledge-wisdom energy; you have to nurture that energy within your own mind.

Why does Mahayana Buddhism teach us to develop a feeling of equanimity for all sentient beings? We often choose just one small thing, one small atom, one single living being, thinking, "This is the one for me; this is the best." Thus, we create extremes of value: we grossly exaggerate the value of the one we like and engender disdain for all the rest. This is not good for you, for your mental peace. Instead, you should examine your behavior, "Why am I doing this? My unrealistic, egocentric mind is polluting my consciousness." Then, by meditating on equanimity—all sentient beings are exactly the same in wanting happiness and not desiring suffering—you can learn to eliminate the extremes of tremendous attachment to one and tremendous aversion to the other. In this way you can easily keep your mind balanced and healthy. Many people have had this experience.

Therefore, Lord Buddha's psychology can be of great help when you're trying to deal with the frustrations that disturb your daily life. Remember that when pleasant feelings arise, desire, craving and attachment follow in their wake; when unpleasant feelings arise, aversion and hatred appear; and when you feel neutral, ignorance, blindness to reality, occupies your mind. If, through these teachings, you can learn the reality of how your feelings arise and how you react to them, your life will be much improved and you will experience much happiness, peace and joy.

Are there any questions?

Q: Buddhism always talks about karma. What is it?
Lama: Karma is your experiences of body and mind. The word itself is Sanskrit; it means cause and effect. Your experiences of mental and physical happiness or unhappiness are the effects of certain causes, but those effects themselves become the causes of future results. One action produces a reaction; that is karma. Both Eastern philosophies and science explain that all matter is interrelated; if you can understand that, you will understand how karma works. All existence, internal and external, does not come about accidentally; the energy of all internal and external phenomena is interdependent. For example, your body's energy is related to the energy of your parents' bodies; their bodies' energy is related to their parents' bodies, and so forth. That sort of evolution is karma.

Q: What is *nirvana* and do many people attain it?
Lama: When you develop your powers of concentration such that you can integrate your mind into single-pointed concentration, you will gradually diminish your ego's emotional reactions until they disappear altogether. At that point, you transcend your ego and dis-

cover an everlasting, blissful, peaceful state of mind. That is what we call nirvana. Many people have attained this state and many more are well on their way to it.

Q: In nirvana, do you cease to exist in a bodily form; does the person disappear?
Lama: No, you still have a form, but it doesn't have an uncontrolled nervous system like the one we have now. And don't worry, when you attain nirvana you still exist, but in a state of perfect happiness. So, try hard to reach it as soon as possible.

Q: Didn't Buddha say that he would never be reborn once he had attained nirvana?
Lama: Perhaps, but what did he mean? He meant that he would not take an uncontrolled rebirth impelled by the energy force of ego, which is the way we samsaric sentient beings are reborn. Instead, he can reincarnate with perfect control, his only purpose being to help mother sentient beings.

Q: You spoke a lot about pleasure and happiness, and I am trying to get clear in my mind the distinction between the two. Are they the same? Can one become attached to pleasure but not to happiness?
Lama: They're the same thing and we get attached to both. What we should aim for is the experience of pleasure without attachment; we should enjoy our feelings of happiness while understanding the nature of the subject, our mind, the object, and our feelings. Someone who has reached nirvana is able to do this.

Q: I would like to clarify the Buddhist meaning of meditation. Am I right in interpreting it as "observing the passage of your mind"?
Lama: Yes, you can think of it that way. As I said before, Buddhist meditation doesn't necessarily mean sitting cross-legged with your eyes closed. Simply observing how your mind is responding to the sense world as you go about your business—walking, talking, shopping, whatever—can be a really perfect meditation and bring a perfect result.

Q: With respect to rebirth, what is it that is reborn?

Lama: When you die, your consciousness separates from your body, enters the intermediate state, and from there it is born into another physical form. We call that rebirth. Physical and mental energy are different from each other. Physical energy is extremely limited, but mental energy always has continuity.

Q: Is it possible for the consciousness to develop in the after-death state or is it only in life that consciousness can evolve?

Lama: During the death process, your consciousness keeps flowing, just like electricity, which comes from the generator but flows continually through different houses, different appliances and so forth, occupying different things. So, it is possible for the consciousness to develop in the intermediate state.

Q: So the mind does not need a physical body to develop?

Lama: Well, there is an intermediate state body, but it's not like ours; it's a very light, psychic body.

Q: When you recite mantras, do you ever concentrate on any of the body's physical organs or do you focus only on your mind? Can you concentrate on your *chakras,* or energy centers?

Lama: It's possible, but you have to remember that there are different methods for different purposes. Don't think that Lord Buddha taught only one thing. Buddhism contains thousands upon thousands, perhaps even countless, methods of meditation, all given in order to suit the varying propensities and dispositions of the infinite individual living beings.

Q: Is the consciousness that develops during our life and leaves when we die a part of some supreme consciousness? Like God or universal consciousness?

Lama: No, it's a very ordinary, simple mind and is in direct continuity with the mind you have right now. The difference is that it has separated from your body and is seeking another. This intermediate state mind is under the control of karma, and is agitated, conflicted and confused. There's no way you can call it higher or supreme.

Q: Are you familiar with the Hindu concepts of *atman* and *brahman?*
Lama: While Hindu philosophy accepts the idea of a soul [atman], Buddhism does not. We completely deny the existence of a self-existent I, or a permanent, independent soul. Every aspect of your body and mind is impermanent: changing, changing, changing.... Buddhists also deny the existence of a permanent hell. Every pain, every pleasure we experience is in a state of constant flux; so transitory, so impermanent, always changing, never lasting. Therefore, recognizing the dissatisfactory nature of our existence and renouncing the world in which transitory sense objects contact transitory sense organs to produce transitory feelings, none of which are worth grasping at, we seek instead the everlasting, eternally joyful realizations of enlightenment or nirvana.

Q: Do you think ritual is as important to the Western person trying to practice Buddhism as it is to the Easterner, who has a feeling for it?
Lama: It depends on what you mean. Actual Buddhist meditation doesn't require you to accompany it with material objects; the only thing that matters is your mind. You don't need to ring bells or wave things about. Is that what you mean by ritual? [Yes.] Good; so, you don't need to worry, and that applies equally to the East as it does to the West. Nevertheless, some people do need these things; different minds need different methods. For example, you wear glasses. They're not the most important thing, but some people need them. For the same reason, the various world religions teach various paths according to the individual abilities and levels of their many and varied followers. Therefore, we cannot say, "This is the one true way. Everybody should follow my path."

Q: Are new methods of practice required in the West today?
Lama: No. No new methods are required. All the methods are there

already; you just need to discover them.

Q: I am trying to understand the relationship in Buddhism between the mind and the body. Is mind more important than body? For example, in the case of tantric monks who do overtone chanting, obviously they develop a part of their body in order to sing, so just how important is the body?

Lama: The mind is the most important thing, but there are some meditation practices that are enhanced by certain physical yoga exercises. Conversely, if your body is sick, that can affect your mind. So, it's also important to keep your body healthy. But if you concern yourself with only the physical and neglect to investigate the reality of your own mind, that's not wise either; it's unbalanced, not realistic. So, I think we all agree that the mind is more important than the body, but at the same time, we cannot forget about the body altogether. I've seen Westerners come to the East for teachings, and when they hear about Tibetan yogis living in the high mountains without food they think, "Oh, fantastic! I want to be just like Milarepa." That's a mistake. If you were born in the West, your body is used to certain specific conditions, so to keep it healthy, you need to create a conducive environment. You can't do a Himalayan trip. Be wise, not extreme.

Q: Is it true that when a human is born his or her mind is pure and innocent?

Lama: As we all know, when you are born, your mind is not too occupied by intellectual complications. But as you get older and start to think, it begins to fill up with so much information, philosophy, "that-this," this is good, that is bad, I should have this, I shouldn't have that…you intellectualize too much, filling your mind with garbage. That certainly makes your mind much worse. Still, that doesn't mean that you were born absolutely pure and that only after the arrival of the intellect did you become negative. It doesn't mean that. Why not? Because if you were fundamentally free of ignorance and attachment, any garbage coming at you would not be able to get in. Unfortunately, we're not like that. Fundamentally, not only are we wide open to whatever intellectual garbage comes our way, but we've got a big welcome sign out. So moment by moment, more and more garbage is piling up in our minds. Therefore, you can't say that children are born with absolutely pure minds. It's wrong. Babies cry because they have feelings. When an unpleasant feeling arises—perhaps they're craving their mother's milk—they cry.

Q: We have this idea of consciousness transmigrating from body to body, from life to life, but if there is continuity of consciousness, why is it that we don't remember our previous lives?

Lama: Too much supermarket information crowding into our minds makes us forget our previous experiences. Even science says that the brain is limited such that new information suppresses the old. They say that, but it's not quite right. What actually happens is that basically, the human mind is mostly unconscious, ignorant, and gets so preoccupied with new experiences that it forgets the old ones. Review the past month: exactly what happened, precisely what feelings did you have, every day? You can't remember, can you? So checking back further, all the way back to the time when you were just a few cells in your mother's womb, then even farther back than that: it's very difficult, isn't it? But if you practice this slowly, slowly, continuously checking within your mind, eventually you'll be able to remember more and more of your previous experiences. Many of us may have had the experience of reacting very strangely to something that has happened and being perplexed by our reaction, which seems not to have been based on any of this life's experiences: "That's weird. Why did I react like that? I've no idea where that came from." That's because it's based on a previous life's experience. Modern psychologists cannot explain such reactions because they don't understand mental continuity, the beginningless nature of each individual's mind. They don't understand that mental reactions can result from impulses that were generated thousands and thousands of years ago. But if you keep investigating your mind through meditation, you will eventually understand all this through your own experience.

Q: Could it be negative to find out about previous lives? Could it be disturbing?

Lama: Well, it could be either a positive or a negative experience. If you *realize* your previous lives, it will be positive. Disturbance comes from ignorance. You should try to realize the characteristic nature of negativity. When you do, the problem's solved. Understanding the nature of negativity stops the problems it brings. Therefore, right understanding is the only solution to both physical and mental problems. You should always check very carefully how you're expending your energy: will it make you happy or not? That's a big responsibility, don't you think? It's your choice: the path of wisdom or the path of ignorance.

Q: What is the meaning of suffering?

Lama: Mental agitation is suffering; dissatisfaction is suffering. Actually, it is very important to understand the various subtle levels of suffering, otherwise people are going to say, "Why does Buddhism say everybody's suffering? I'm happy." When Lord Buddha talked about suffering, he didn't mean just the pain of a wound or the kind of mental anguish that we often experience. We say that we're happy, but if we check our happiness more closely, we'll find that there's still plenty of dissatisfaction in our minds. From the Buddhist point of view, simply the fact that we can't control our minds is mental suffering; in fact, that's worse than the various physical sufferings we experience. Therefore, when Buddhism talks about suffering, it's emphasizing the mental level much more than the physical, and that's why, in practical terms, Buddhist teachings are basically applied psychology. Buddhism teaches the nature of suffering at the mental level and the methods for its eradication.

Q: Why do we all experience suffering and what do we learn from it?

Lama: That's so simple, isn't it? Why are you suffering? Because you're too involved in acting out of ignorance and grasping with attachment. You learn from suffering by realizing where it comes from and exactly what it is that makes you suffer. In our infinite previous lives we have had so many experiences but we still haven't learned that much. Many people think that they're learning from their experiences, but they're not. There are infinite past experiences in their unconscious but they still know nothing about their own true nature.

Q: Why do we have the opportunity to be attached?
Lama: Because we're hallucinating; we're not seeing the reality of either the subject or the object. When you understand the nature of an object of attachment, the subjective mind of attachment automatically disappears. It's the foggy mind, the mind that's attracted to an object and paints a distorted projection onto it, that makes you suffer. That's all. It's really quite simple.

Q: I've seen Tibetan images of wrathful deities, but although they were fierce-looking, they didn't look evil. That made me wonder whether or not Buddhism emphasizes evil and bad things.
Lama: Buddhism never emphasizes the existence of external evil. Evil is a projection of your mind. If evil exists, it's within you. There's no outside evil to fear. Wrathful deities are emanations of enlightened wisdom and serve to help people who have a lot of uncontrolled anger. In meditation, the angry person transforms his anger into wisdom, which is then visualized as a wrathful deity; thus the energy of his anger is digested by wisdom. Briefly, that's how the method works.

Q: What do you feel about a person killing another person in self-defense? Do you think people have the right to protect themselves, even at the expense of the aggressor's life?
Lama: In most cases of killing in self-defense, it's still done out of uncontrolled anger. You should protect yourself as best you can without killing the other. For example, if you attack me, I'm responsible

to protect myself, but without killing you.

Q: If killing me was the only way you could stop me, would you do it?
Lama: Then it would be better that you kill me.

Well, if there are no further questions, I won't keep you any longer.
Thank you very much for everything.

Christchurch, New Zealand
14 June 1975

Part Two

Make Your Mind an Ocean

Aspects of Buddhist Psychology

EDITOR'S INTRODUCTION

In the LAMA YESHE WISDOM ARCHIVE's first book, Lama Yeshe's *Becoming Your Own Therapist*, I mentioned the unique qualities of Lama Yeshe's teachings. *Make Your Mind an Ocean* again makes evident just how special Lama's teachings were.

The talks in this section are on the general topic of the mind and were given during Lama Yeshe's and Lama Zopa Rinpoche's second world tour, in 1975. I had the great honor of accompanying the Lamas on this tour and was present at all these discourses. Most of the people who attended were new to Buddhism and had never seen a Tibetan lama before, a situation quite different from what we find today. As ever, Lama's timeless wisdom shines through, and his teachings are as relevant today as they were back then.

Two of these talks were lunchtime lectures at Melbourne and Latrobe Universities. The latter started a bit late, so there was no time to finish with the usual question and answer session that Lama liked so much. The chapter "Make Your Mind an Ocean" was an evening lecture given to the general public and attended by several hundred people.

Of greatest interest, perhaps, is "A Buddhist Approach to Mental Illness." Here Lama met with a group of psychiatrists at Prince Henry's Hospital, which was at that time a teaching hospital connected with Monash University Medical School. Prior to that it had been affiliated with Melbourne University, and Prince Henry's was where I studied my clinical medicine and worked for several years after graduation. Thus, several of the psychiatrists with whom Lama met that afternoon were former teachers and colleagues of mine, and apart from anything else, I was interested to observe their reaction to my outer transformation (I was in monk's robes at the time). The hospital was demolished a few years ago; the last time I drove by it was but a hole in the ground, a symbol of how much has changed since those halcyon days. Anyway, these doctors were delighted to meet and question Lama, and this historic exchange underscores the difference between Western and Buddhist concepts of mental health.

I would like to thank Rand Engel, Victoria Fremont, Christina Russo and Wendy Cook for their excellent editorial input, which greatly improved the way these teachings read.

Your Mind is Your Religion

When I talk about mind, I'm not just talking about my mind, my trip. I'm talking about the mind of each and every universal living being.

The way we live, the way we think—everything is dedicated to material pleasure. We consider sense objects to be of utmost importance and materialistically devote ourselves to whatever makes us happy, famous or popular. Even though all this comes from our mind, we are so totally preoccupied by external objects that we never look within, we never question why we find them so interesting.

As long as we exist, our mind is an inseparable part of us. As a result, we are always up and down. It is not our body that goes up and down, it's our mind—this mind whose way of functioning we do not understand. Therefore, sometimes we have to examine ourselves—not just our body, but our mind. After all, it is our mind that is always telling us what to do. We have to know our own psychology, or, in religious terminology, perhaps, our inner nature. Anyway, no matter what we call it, we have to know our own mind.

Don't think that examining and knowing the nature of your mind is just an Eastern trip. That's a wrong conception. It's your trip. How can you separate your body, or your self-image, from your mind? It's impossible. You think you are an independent person, free to travel the world, enjoying everything. Despite what you think, you are not free. I'm not saying that you are under the control of someone else. It's your own uncontrolled mind, your own attachment, that oppresses you. If you discover how you oppress yourself, your uncontrolled mind will disappear. Knowing your own mind is the solution to all your problems.

One day the world looks so beautiful; the next day it looks terrible. How can you say that? Scientifically, it's impossible that the world can change so radically. It's your mind that causes these appearances. This is not religious dogma; your up and down is not religious dogma. I'm not talking about religion; I'm talking about the way you lead your daily life, which is what sends you up and down. Other people and your environment don't change radically; it's your mind. I hope you understand that.

Similarly, one person thinks that the world is beautiful and people are wonderful and kind, while another thinks that everything and everyone are horrible. Who is right? How do you explain that scientifically? It's just their individual mind's projection of the sense world. You think, "Today is like this, tomorrow is like that; this man is like this; that woman is like that." But where is that absolutely fixed, forever-beautiful woman? Who is that absolutely forever-handsome man? They are non-existent—they are simply creations of your own mind.

Do not expect material objects to satisfy you or to make your life perfect; it's impossible. How can you be satisfied by even vast amounts of material objects? How will sleeping with hundreds of different people satisfy you? It will never happen. Satisfaction comes from the mind.

If you don't know your own psychology, you might ignore what's going on in your mind until it breaks down and you go completely crazy. People go mad through lack of inner wisdom, through their inability to examine their own minds. They cannot explain themselves to themselves; they don't know how to talk to themselves. Thus they are constantly preoccupied with all these external objects, while within, their minds are running down until they finally crack. They are ignorant of their internal world, and their minds are totally unified with ignorance instead of being awake and engaged in self-analysis. Examine your own mental attitudes. Become your own therapist.

You are intelligent; you know that material objects alone cannot bring you satisfaction, but you don't have to embark on some emotional, religious trip to examine your own mind. Some people think that they do; that this kind of self-analysis is something spiritual or religious. It's not necessary to classify yourself as a follower of this or that religion or philosophy, to put yourself into some religious category. But if you want to be happy, you have to check the way you lead your life. Your mind is your religion.

When you check your mind, do not rationalize or push. Relax. Do not be upset when problems arise. Just be aware of them and where they come from; know their root. Introduce the problem to yourself: "Here is this kind of problem. How has it become a problem? What kind of mind has made it a problem? What kind of mind feels that it's a problem?" When you check thoroughly, the problem will automatically disappear. That's so simple, isn't it? You don't have to believe in something. Don't believe anything! All the same, you can't say, "I don't believe I have a mind." You can't reject your mind. You can say, "I reject Eastern things"—I agree. But can you reject yourself? Can you deny your head, your nose? You cannot deny your mind. Therefore, treat yourself wisely and try to discover the true source of satisfaction.

When you were a child you loved and craved ice-cream, chocolate and cake, and thought, "When I grow up, I'll have all the ice-cream, chocolate and cake I want; then I'll be happy." Now you have as much ice-cream, chocolate and cake as you want, but you're bored. You decide that since this doesn't make you happy you'll get a car, a house, television, a husband or wife—then you'll be happy. Now you have everything, but your car is a problem, your house is a problem, your husband or wife is a problem, your children are a problem. You realize, "Oh, this is not satisfaction."

What, then, is satisfaction? Go through all this mentally and check; it's very important. Examine your life from childhood to the present. This is analytical meditation: "At that time my mind was like that; now my mind is like this. It has changed this way, that way." Your mind has changed so many times but have you reached any conclusion as to what really makes you happy? My interpretation is that you are lost. You know your way around the city, how to get home, where to buy chocolate, but still you are lost—you can't find your goal. Check honestly—isn't this so?

Lord Buddha says that all you have to know is what you are, how you exist. You don't have to believe in anything. Just understand your mind: how it works, how attachment and desire arise, how ignorance arises, and where emotions come from. It is sufficient to know the nature of all that; that alone can bring you happiness and peace. Thus, your life can change completely; everything can turn upside down. What you once interpreted as horrible can become beautiful.

If I told you that all you were living for was chocolate and ice-cream, you'd think I was crazy. "No! no!" your arrogant mind would say. But look deeper into your life's purpose. Why are you here? To be well liked? To become famous? To accumulate possessions? To be attractive to others? I'm not exaggerating—check for yourself, then you'll see. Through thorough examination you can realize that dedicating your entire life to seeking happiness through chocolate and ice-cream completely nullifies the significance of your having been born human. Birds and dogs have similar aims. Shouldn't your goals in life be higher than those of dogs and chickens?

I'm not trying to decide your life for you, but you check up. It's better to have an integrated life than to live in mental disorder. A disorderly life is not worthwhile, beneficial to neither yourself nor others. What *are* you living for—chocolate? Steak? Perhaps you think, "Of course I don't live for food. I'm an educated person." But education also comes from the mind. Without the mind, what is education, what is philosophy? Philosophy is just the creation of someone's mind, a few thoughts strung together in a certain way. Without the mind there's no philosophy, no doctrine, no university subjects. All these things are mind-made.

How do you check your mind? Just watch how it perceives or interprets any object that it encounters. Observe what feelings—comfortable or uncomfortable—arise. Then check, "When I perceive this kind of view, this feeling arises, that emotion comes; I discriminate in such a way. Why?" This is how to check your mind; that's all. It's very simple.

When you check your own mind properly, you stop blaming others for your problems. You recognize that your mistaken actions come from your own defiled, deluded mind. When you are preoccupied with external, material objects, you blame them and other people for your problems. Projecting that deluded view onto external phenomena makes you miserable. When you begin to realize your wrong-conception view, you begin to realize the nature of your own mind and to put an end to your problems forever.

Is all this very new for you? It's not. Whenever you are going to do anything, you first check it out and then make your decision. You already do this; I'm not suggesting anything new. The difference is that you don't do it enough. You have to do more checking. This doesn't mean sitting alone in some corner contemplating your navel—you can be checking your mind all the time, even while talking or working with other people. Do you think that examining the mind is only for those who are on an Eastern trip? Don't think that way.

Realize that the nature of your mind is different from that of the flesh and bone of your physical body. Your mind is like a mirror, reflecting everything without discrimination. If you have understanding-wisdom, you can control the kind of reflection that you allow into the mirror of your mind. If you totally ignore what is happening in your mind, it will reflect whatever garbage it encounters—things that make you psychologically sick. Your checking-wisdom should distinguish between reflections that are beneficial and those that bring psychological problems. Eventually, when you realize the true nature of subject and object, all your problems will vanish.

Some people think they are religious, but what is religious? If you do not examine your own nature, do not gain knowledge-wisdom, how are you religious? Just the idea that you are religious—"I am Buddhist, Jewish, whatever"—does not help at all. It does not help you; it does not help others. In order to really help others, you need to gain knowledge-wisdom.

The greatest problems of humanity are psychological, not material. From birth to death, people are continuously under the control of their mental sufferings. Some people never keep watch on their minds when things are going well, but when something goes wrong—an accident or some other terrible experience—they immediately say, "God, please help me." They call themselves religious but it's a joke. In happiness or sorrow, a serious practitioner maintains constant awareness of God and one's own nature. You're not being realistic or even remotely religious if, when you are having a good time, surrounded by chocolate and preoccupied by worldly sense pleasures, you forget yourself, and turn to God only when something awful happens.

No matter which of the many world religions we consider, their interpretation of God or Buddha and so forth is simply words and mind; these two alone. Therefore, words don't matter so much. What you have to realize is that everything—good and bad, every philosophy and doctrine—comes from mind. The mind is very powerful. Therefore, it requires firm guidance. A powerful jet plane needs a good pilot; the pilot of your mind should be the wisdom that understands its nature. In that way, you can direct your powerful mental energy to benefit your life instead of letting it run about uncontrollably like a mad elephant, destroying yourself and others.

I don't need to say much more. I think you understand what I'm talking about. At this point a little dialog would be more useful. Ask questions; I'll try to answer. Remember that you don't have to agree with what I say. You have to understand my attitude, my mind. If you don't like what I've been saying, please contradict me. I like people to argue with me. I'm not a dictator: "You people should do this; you people should do that." I can't tell you what to do. I make suggestions; what I want is for you to check up. If you do that, I'll be satisfied. So tell me if you disagree with what I've said.

Q: How do you check up on your own mind? How do you do it?
Lama: A simple way of checking up on your own mind is to investigate how you perceive things, how you interpret your experiences. Why do you have so many different feelings about your boyfriend even during the course of one day? In the morning you feel good

about him, in the afternoon, kind of foggy; why is that? Has your boyfriend changed that radically from morning to afternoon? No, there's been no radical change, so why do you feel so differently about him? That's the way to check.

Q: If you can't trust your mind to make a decision, can you leave it to something outside? Like telling yourself, "If such and such happens, I'll go here; if something else happens, I'll go there."
Lama: Before you do anything, you should ask yourself why you are doing it, what is your purpose; what course of action you are embarking on. If the path ahead seems troublesome, perhaps you shouldn't take it; if it looks worthwhile, you can probably proceed. First, check up. Don't act without knowing what's in store for you.

Q: What's a lama?
Lama: Good question. From the Tibetan point of view, a lama is someone who is extremely well educated in the internal world and knows not only the present mind but also the past and the future. Psychologically speaking, a lama can see where he has come from and where he's going. He also has the power to control himself and the ability to offer psychological advice to others. Tibetans would con-sider anyone like that to be a lama.

Q: What would be the equivalent of a lama in the West?
Lama: I don't know that we have the exact equivalent here. It could be some kind of combination of priest, psychologist and doctor. But as I just said, a lama has realized the true nature of his own and others' minds and can offer perfect solutions to others' mental problems. I'm not criticizing them, but I doubt that many Western psychologists have the same degree of understanding of the mind or the emotional problems that people experience. Sometimes they offer somewhat poor quality, superficial explanations for the problems people are going through, such as, "When you were a child your mother did this, your father did that..." I disagree; it's not true. You can't blame your parents for your problems like that. Of course,

environmental factors can contribute to difficulties, but the principal cause is always within you; the basic problem is never outside. I don't know, but perhaps Western doctors are too afraid to interpret things in this way. Also, I have met many priests, some of whom are my friends, but they tend not to deal too much with the here and now. Instead of focusing on practical ways of coping with everyday uncertainties, they emphasize religious considerations such as God, faith and so forth. But people today tend to be skeptical and often reject the help that some priests can offer.

Q: How does meditation help you make decisions?
Lama: Meditation works because it is not a method that requires you to believe in something but rather one that you can put into action for yourself. You check, or watch, your own mind. If someone's giving you a hard time and your ego starts to hurt, instead of reacting, just take a look at what's going on. Think of how sound is simply coming out of the other person's mouth, entering your ear, and causing pain in your heart. If you think about this in the right way, it will make you laugh; you will see how ridiculous it is to get upset by something so insubstantial. Then your problem will disappear—poof! Just like that. By practicing in this way, you will discover through your own experience how meditation helps and how it offers satisfactory solutions to all your problems. Meditation is not words, it's wisdom.

Q: Lama, could you please talk a little about karma.
Lama: Sure: *you are karma.* It's that simple. Actually, karma is a Sanskrit word that, roughly translated, means cause and effect. What does that mean? Yesterday something happened in your mind; today you experience the effect. Or, your environment: you have certain parents, you live in a certain situation, all that has an effect on you. As you go through life, every day, everything you do, all the time, within your mind there's a constant chain of cause and reaction, cause and reaction; that's karma. As long as you're in your body, interacting with the sense world, discriminating this is good,

that is bad, your mind is automatically creating karma, cause and effect. Karma is not just theoretical philosophy, it's science, Buddhist science. Karma explains how life evolves; form and feeling, color and sensation, discrimination; your entire life, what you are, where you come from, how you keep going, your relationship with your mind. Karma is Buddhism's scientific explanation of evolution. So, even though karma is a Sanskrit word, actually, *you are* karma, your whole life is controlled by karma, you live within the energy field of karma. Your energy interacts with another energy, then another, and another, and that's how your entire life unfolds. Physically, mentally, it's all karma. Therefore, karma isn't something you have to believe in. Because of the characteristic nature of your mind and body, you are constantly circling through the six realms of cyclic existence, whether you believe in karma or not. In the physical universe, when everything comes together—earth, sea, the four elements, heat and so forth—effects automatically result; there's no need for belief to know this happens. It's the same thing in your internal universe, especially when you're in contact with the sense world; you're constantly reacting. For example, last year you enjoyed delicious chocolate with much attachment but haven't had any since, so you miss it badly, "Oh, I'd really love some chocolate." You remember your previous experience of chocolate; that memory causes you to crave and grasp for more. That reaction to your previous experience is karma; the experience is the cause, the missing is the result. It's actually quite simple.

Q: What is your purpose in life?
Lama: You're asking me about my purpose in life? That's something for me to check for myself, but if I had to reply, I'd say my purpose is to dedicate myself as much as I possibly can to the welfare of others, while trying to be of benefit to myself as well. I can't say that I'm succeeding in any of this, but those are my aims.

Q: Is the mind different from the soul? When you speak of solving the problems of the mind, do you mean that the mind is the problem and not the soul?

Lama: Philosophically, the soul can be interpreted in a number of ways. In Christianity and Hinduism, the soul is different from the mind and is considered to be something permanent and self-existent. In my opinion, there's no such thing. In Buddhist terminology, the soul, mind or whatever you call it is ever-changing, impermanent. I don't really make a distinction between mind and soul, but within yourself you can't find anything that's permanent or self-existent. With respect to mental problems, don't think that the mind is totally negative; it's the uncontrolled mind that causes problems. If you develop the right kind of wisdom and thereby recognize the nature of the uncontrolled mind, it will automatically disappear. But until you do, the uncontrolled mind will completely dominate you.

Q: I've heard many times that many Westerners can grasp the philosophy of Tibetan Buddhism intellectually but have difficulty in putting it into practice. It makes sense to them but they can't integrate it with their lives. What do you think the block is?

Lama: That's a great question, thank you. Tibetan Buddhism teaches you to overcome your dissatisfied mind, but to do that you have to make an effort. To put our techniques into your own experience, you have to go slowly, gradually. You can't just jump right in the deep end. It takes time and we expect you to have trouble at first. But if you take it easy it gets less and less difficult as time goes by.

Q: What is our mind's true nature and how do we go about recognizing it?

Lama: There are two aspects to the mind's nature, the relative and the absolute. The relative is the mind that perceives and functions in the sense world. We also call that mind dualistic and because of what I describe as its "that-this" perception, it is totally agitated in nature. However, by transcending the dualistic mind, you can unify your view. At that time you realize the absolute true nature of the mind, which is totally beyond the duality. In dealing with the sense world in our normal, everyday, mundane life, two things always appear. The appearance of two things always creates a problem. It's like children—one alone is OK, two together always make trouble. Similarly, as our five senses interpret the world and supply dualistic information to our mind, our mind grasps at that view, and that automatically causes conflict and agitation. This is the complete opposite of the experience of inner peace and freedom. Therefore, by reaching beyond that you will experience perfect peace. Now, this is just a short reply to what you asked and perhaps it's unsatisfactory, because it's a big question. What I've said is merely a simple introduction to a profound topic. However, if you have some background in this subject, my answer might satisfy you.

Q: When you check your mind, does it always tell you the truth?
Lama: No, not necessarily. Sometimes your wrong conceptions answer. You shouldn't listen to them. Instead, you have to tell yourself, I'm not satisfied with what that mind says; I want a better answer. You have to keep checking more and more deeply until your wisdom responds. But it's good to question; if you don't ask questions, you'll never get any answers. But you shouldn't ask emotionally, Oh, what's that, what's that, what's that? I have to find out; I have to know. If you have a question, write it down; think about it carefully. Gradually the right answer will come. It takes time. If you don't get an answer today, stick the question on your fridge. If you question strongly, answers will come, sometimes even in dreams. Why will you get answers? Because your basic nature is wisdom. Don't think that you're hopelessly ignorant. Human nature has both positive and negative aspects.

Q: What is your definition of a guru?
Lama: A guru is a person who can really show you the true nature of your mind and who knows the perfect remedies for your psychological problems. Someone who doesn't know his own mind can never know others' minds and therefore cannot be a guru. Such a person can never solve other people's problems. You have to be extremely

careful before taking someone on as a guru; there are many impostors around. Westerners are sometimes too trusting. Someone comes along, "I'm a lama, I'm a yogi; I can give you knowledge," and earnest young Westerners think, "I'm sure he can teach me something. I'm going to follow him." This can really get you into trouble. I've heard of many cases of people being taken in by charlatans. Westerners tend to believe too easily. Eastern people are much more skeptical. Take your time; relax; check up.

Q: Does humility always accompany wisdom?
Lama: Yes. It's good to be as humble as possible. If you can act with both humility and wisdom all the time, your life will be wonderful. You will respect everybody.

Q: Are there exceptions to that rule? I've seen posters for one spiritual leader where it says, "I, at whose feet all people bow." Could someone who makes a statement like that be wise?
Lama: Well, it's hard to say, just like that. The point is to be as careful as you can. Our minds are funny. Sometimes we are skeptical of things that are really worthwhile and completely accepting of things that we should avoid. Try to avoid extremes and follow the middle way, checking with wisdom wherever you go. That's the most important thing.

Q: Why is there this difference between Easterners and Westerners that you mentioned?
Lama: The differences may not be all that great. Westerners might be slightly more complicated intellectually, but basically human beings are all the same; most of the time we all want to enjoy and are preoccupied by pleasures of the senses. It's at the intellectual level that our characters may differ. The differences in relation to following gurus are probably due to Asian people having had more experience in this.

Q: Is it more difficult to achieve wisdom in the West than in the

East because in the West we are surrounded by too many distractions, our minds talk too much about the past, the future, and we seem to be under so much pressure? Do we have to close ourselves off completely or what?

Lama: I cannot say that gaining knowledge-wisdom in the West is more difficult than in the East. Actually, gaining wisdom, understanding your own nature, is an individual thing. You can't say it's easier in the East than in the West. Nor can you say that to develop knowledge-wisdom you have to renounce the Western material life. You don't have to give it all up. Instead of radically abandoning everything, try to develop the outlook, "I need these things, but I can't say they're all I need." The problem comes when grasping and attachment dominate your mind and you put all your faith in other people and material possessions. External objects aren't the problem; the problem is the grasping mind that tells you, "I can't live without this." You can lead a life of incredible luxury but at the same time be completely detached from your possessions. The pleasure you derive from them is much greater if you enjoy them without attachment. If you can manage that, your life will be perfect. As Westerners you have the advantage of getting all these things without too much effort. In the East we really have to struggle to achieve some material comfort. As a result, there's a tendency to cling much more strongly to our possessions, which only results in more suffering. Either way, the problem is always attachment. Try simultaneously to be free of attachment while having it all.

I hope I have answered your questions. Thank you all so much.

Melbourne University
Melbourne, Australia
25 March 1975

A Buddhist Approach to Mental Illness

I was born near Lhasa, the capital of Tibet, and educated at Sera Monastic University, one of the three great monasteries in Lhasa. There they taught us how to bring an end to human problems—not so much the problems people face in their relationship to the external environment, but the internal, mental problems we all face. That was what I studied—Buddhist psychology; how to treat mental illness.

For the past ten years I have been working with Westerners, experimenting to see if Buddhist psychology also works for the Western mind. In my experience, it has been extremely effective. Recently, some of these students invited me to the West to give lectures and meditation courses, so here I am.

We lamas think that the main point is that human problems arise primarily from the mind, not from the external environment. But rather than my talking about things that you might find irrelevant, perhaps it would be better for you to ask specific questions so that I can address directly the issues that are of most interest to you.

Dr. Stan Gold: Lama, thank you very much for coming. Could I start by asking what you mean by "mental illness"?
Lama: By mental illness I mean the kind of mind that does not see reality; a mind that tends to either exaggerate or underestimate the qualities of the person or object it perceives, which always causes problems to arise. In the West, you wouldn't consider this to be mental illness, but Western psychology's interpretation is too narrow. If someone is obviously emotionally disturbed, you consider that to be a problem, but if someone has a fundamental inability to see reality, to understand his or her own true nature, you don't. Not

knowing your own basic mental attitude is a huge problem.

Human problems are more than just emotional distress or disturbed relationships. In fact, those are tiny problems. It's as if there's this huge ocean of problems below, but all we see are the small waves on the surface. We focus on those—"Oh, yes, that's a big problem"—while ignoring the actual cause, the dissatisfied nature of the human mind. It's difficult to see, but we consider people who are unaware of the nature of their dissatisfied mind to be mentally ill; their minds are not healthy.

Q: Lama Yeshe, how do you go about treating mental illness? How do you help people with mental illness?
Lama: Yes, good, wonderful. My way of treating mental illness is to try to have the person analyze the basic nature of his own problem. I try to show him the true nature of his mind so that with his own mind he can understand his own problems. If he can do that, he can solve his own problems himself. I don't believe that I can solve his problems by simply talking to him a little. That might make him feel a bit better, but it's very transient relief. The root of his problems reaches deep into his mind; as long as it's there, changing circumstances will cause more problems to emerge.

My method is to have him check his own mind in order to gradually see its true nature. I've had the experience of giving someone a little advice and having him think, "Oh, great, my problem's gone; Lama solved it with just a few words," but that's a fabrication. He's just making it up. There's no way you can understand your own mental problems without your becoming *your* own psychologist. It's impossible.

Q: How do you help people understand their problems? How do you go about it?
Lama: I try to show them the psychological aspect of their nature, how to check their own minds. Once they know this, they can check and solve their own problems. I try to teach them an approach.

Q: What, precisely, is the method that you teach for looking at the mind's true nature?
Lama: Basically it's a form of checking, or analytical, knowledge-wisdom.

Q: Is it a kind of meditation?
Lama: Yes; analytical, or checking, meditation.

Q: How do you do that? How do you teach somebody to check?
Lama: Let me give you an example. Say I have a good feeling about somebody. I have to ask myself, "Why do I feel good about this person? What makes me feel this way?" By investigating this I might find that it's just because he was nice to me once, or that there's some other similar small, illogical reason. "I love him because he did this or that." It's the same thing if I feel bad about someone; I don't like him because he did such and such. But if you look more deeply to see if those good or bad qualities really exist within the person you may see that your discrimination of friend or enemy is based on very superficial, illogical reasoning. You're basing your judgment on insignificant qualities, not on the totality of the other person's being. You see some quality you label as good or bad, perhaps something the person said or did, and then exaggerate it out of all proportion. Then you become agitated by what you perceive. Through checking you can see that there's no reason to discriminate in the way that you do; it only keeps you fettered, uptight and in suffering. This kind of checking analyzes not the other person but your own mind, in order to see how you feel and to determine what kind of discriminating mind makes you feel that way. This is a fundamentally different approach to analysis from the Western one, which focuses excessively on external factors and not enough on the part played by the mind in people's experience.

Q: So you say that the problem lies more within the person and don't agree with the point of view that it is society that makes people sick?

Lama: Yes. For example, I have met many Western people who've had problems with society. They're angry with society, with their parents, with everything. When they understand the psychology I teach, they think, "Ridiculous! I've always blamed society, but actually the *real* problem has been inside of me all along." Then they become courteous human beings, respectful of society, their parents, their teachers and all other people. You can't blame society for our problems.

Q: Why do people mix things up like that?
Lama: It's because they don't know their own true nature. The environment, ideas and philosophies can be contributory causes, but primarily, problems come from one's own mind. Of course, the way society is organized can agitate some people, but the issues are usually small. Unfortunately, people tend to exaggerate them and get upset. This is how it is with society, but anyone who thinks the world can exist without it is dreaming.

Q: Lama, what do you find in the ocean of a person's nature?
Lama: When I use that expression I'm saying that people's problems are like an ocean, but we see only the superficial waves. We don't see what lies beneath them. "Oh, I have a problem with him. If I get rid of him I'll solve my problems." It's like looking at electrical appliances without understanding that it's the underlying electricity that makes them function.

Q: What kind of problems do we find below the waves?
Lama: Dissatisfaction. The dissatisfied mind is the fundamental element of human nature. We're dissatisfied with ourselves; we're dissatisfied with the outside world. That dissatisfaction is like an ocean.

Q: Do you ask the other person questions about himself or how he feels to help him understand himself?
Lama: Sometimes we do, but usually we don't. Some people have quite specific problems; in such cases it can help to know exactly

what those problems are so that we can offer precise solutions. But it's not usually necessary because basically, everybody's problems are the same.

Q: How much time do you spend talking with that person to find out about his problem and how to deal with it? As you know, in Western psychiatry, we spend a great deal of time with patients to help them discover the nature of their problems for themselves. Do you do the same thing or do you do it differently?

Lama: Our methods don't require us to spend much time with people individually. We explain the fundamental nature of problems and the possibility of transcending them; then we teach basic techniques of working with problems. They practice these techniques; after a while we check to see what their experience has been.

Q: You're saying that basically, everybody has the same problems?

Lama: Yes, right. East, West, it's basically the same thing. But in the West, people have to be clinically ill before you'll say that they're sick. That's too superficial for us. According to Lord Buddha's psychology and lamas' experience, sickness runs deeper than just the overt expression of clinical symptoms. As long as the ocean of dissatisfaction remains within you, the slightest change in the environment can be enough to bring out a problem. As far as we're concerned, even being susceptible to future problems means that your mind is not healthy. All of us here are basically the same, in that our minds are dissatisfied. As a result, a tiny change in our external circumstances can make us sick. Why? Because the basic problem is within our minds. It's much more important to eradicate the basic problem than to spend all our time trying to deal with superficial, emotional ones. This approach doesn't cease our continual experience of problems; it merely substitutes a new problem for the one we believe we've just solved.

Q: Is my basic problem the same as his basic problem?

Lama: Yes, everybody's basic problem is what we call ignorance—

not understanding the nature of the dissatisfied mind. As long you have this kind of mind, you're in the same boat as everybody else. This inability to see reality is not an exclusively Western problem or an exclusively Eastern problem. It's a human problem.

Q: The basic problem is not knowing the nature of your mind?
Lama: Right, yes.

Q: And everybody's mind has the same nature?
Lama: Yes, the same nature.

Q: Each person has the same basic problem?
Lama: Yes, but there are differences. For example, a hundred years ago, people in the West had certain kinds of problems. Largely through technological development, they solved many of them, but now different problems have arisen in their stead. That's what I'm saying. New problems replace the old ones, but they're still problems, because the basic problem remains. The basic problem is like an ocean; the ones we try to solve are just the waves. It's the same in the East. In India, problems people experience in the villages are different from those experienced by people who live in the capital, New Delhi, but they're still problems. East, West, the basic problem is the same.

Q: Lama, as I understand it, you said that the basic problem is that individuals lose touch with their own nature. How do we lose touch with our own nature? Why does it happen?
Lama: One reason is that we are preoccupied with what's going on outside of ourselves. We are so interested in what's going on in the sense world that we do not take the time to examine what's going on in our minds. We never ask ourselves why the sense world is so interesting, why things appear as they do, why we respond to them as we do. I'm not saying we should ignore the outside world, but we should expend at least an equal amount of energy analyzing our relationship with it. If we can comprehend the nature of both the subject and the

object, then we can really put an end to our problems. You might feel that materially your life is perfect, but you can still ask yourself, "Does this really satisfy me? Is this all there is?" You can check your mind, "Where does satisfaction really come from?" If you understand that satisfaction does not depend only on external things, you can enjoy both material possessions and peace of mind.

Q: Is the nature of each person's satisfaction different or is it the same for people in general?

Lama: Relatively speaking, each individual has his or her own way of thinking, feeling and discriminating; therefore each person's enjoyment is an individual thing. Relatively. But if you check more deeply, if you look into the profound, unchangeable, more lasting levels of feeling, happiness and joy, you will see that everybody can attain identical levels of enjoyment. In the relative, mundane world we think, "My interests and pleasures are such and such, therefore I have to have this, this and this. If I find myself in so and so circumstances, I'll be miserable." Relatively, our experiences are individual; each of us discriminates in our own way. But absolutely, we can experience an identical level of happiness.

Q: Lama, do you solve people's problems by getting them to withdraw into meditation or cut themselves off from the outside world? Is this the way you treat people?

Lama: Not necessarily. People should be totally aware of both what's going on in their own minds and how their minds are relating to the outside world, what effect the environment is having on their minds. You can't close your life off from the world; you have to face it; you have to be open to everything.

Q: Is your treatment always successful?

Lama: No. Not necessarily.

Q: What makes it unsuccessful in certain cases?

Lama: Sometimes there's a problem in communication; people misunderstand what I'm saying. Perhaps people don't have the patience to put the methods I recommend into action. It takes time to treat the dissatisfied mind. Changing the mind isn't like painting a house. You can change the color of a house in an hour. It takes a lot longer than that to transform an attitude of mind.

Q: What sort of time are you talking about? Months? Years?
Lama: It depends on the individual and the kind of problem we're talking about. If you're having a problem with your parents, maybe you can solve it in a month. But changing and overcoming the fundamentally dissatisfied mind can take many, many years. The waves are easy; the ocean is more difficult. Thank you, that was a very good question.

Q: Do you have any process by which you select the people that you might try to help?
Lama: No, we have no process of selection.

Q: People just come to you?
Lama: Yes. Anybody can come. Irrespective of color, race, class or gender, all human beings have the same potential to solve their problems. There's no problem that cannot be solved by human wisdom. If you are wise, you can solve them all.

Q: What about people who are not so wise?
Lama: Then you have to teach people how to be wise. Wisdom isn't intuitive; you have to open people's minds to it.

Q: Can you help children to solve problems in this way?
Lama: That's definitely possible. But with children you can't always intellectualize. Sometimes you have to show them things through art or by your actions. Sometimes it's not so wise to tell them to do this or do that.

Q: Lama, what sort of advice would you give parents to help their children know their inner nature?

Lama: First I'd probably say it's better not to intellectualize verbally. Acting correctly and creating a peaceful environment are much more likely to be effective. If you do, children will learn automatically. Even tiny children pick up on vibrations. I remember that when I was a small child, when my parents argued, I felt terrible; it was painful. You don't need to tell children too much but rather behave properly, peacefully and gently, and create a good environment. That's all; especially when they're too small to understand language.

Q: How important is the body in human happiness?
Lama: If you want to be happy, it's very important for your body to be healthy, because of the close link between your physical nervous system and your mind. A disturbance in your nervous system will cause a disturbance in your mind; changes in your body cause changes in your mind. There's a strong connection between the two.

Q: Do you have any advice with respect to diet or sexual behavior in keeping the body healthy?
Lama: Both can be important. Of course, we're all different, so you can't say that the same diet will suit everybody. As individuals, our bodies are habituated to particular diets, so radical dietary changes can shock our systems. Also, too much sexual activity can weaken our bodies, which in turn can weaken our minds, our power of concentration or penetrative wisdom.

Q: What is too much?
Lama: Again, that depends on the individual. It's not the same for everybody. Each person's power of body varies; check through your own experience.

Q: Why are we here? What is our reason for living?
Lama: As long as we're attached to the sense world, we're attached to our bodies, so we have to live in them.

Q: But where am I going? Do I have to go anywhere?

Lama: Yes, of course, you have no choice. You're impermanent, therefore you have to go. Your body is made up of the four ever-changing elements of earth, water, fire and air. When they're in balance, you grow properly and remain healthy. But if one of them gets out of balance with the rest, it can cause chaos in your body and end your life.

Q: And what happens then? Do we reincarnate?

Lama: Yes, we do. Your mind, or consciousness, is different from your physical body, your flesh and blood. When you die, you leave your body behind and your mind goes into a new one. Since beginningless time we've been dying and being reborn into one different body after another. That's what we understand. Lord Buddha's psychology teaches that at the relative level, the characteristic nature of the mind is quite different from that of the physical body.

Q: Do we live in order to continually improve ourselves? When you're an old man, will you be better than you are now?

Lama: You can never be sure of that. Sometimes old men are worse than children. It depends on how much wisdom you have. Some children are wiser than adults. You need wisdom to make that kind of progress during your life.

Q: If you understand yourself better in this life, do you improve in the next?

Lama: Definitely. The better you understand the nature of your mind in this life, the better your next life will be. Even in this life, if you understand your own nature well today, next month your experiences will be better.

Q: Lama, what does *nirvana* mean?

Lama: Nirvana is a Sanskrit word that means freedom, or liberation. Inner liberation. It means that your heart is no longer bound by the uncontrolled, unsubdued, dissatisfied mind, not tied by attachment. When you realize the absolute nature of your mind, you free yourself from bondage and are able to find enjoyment without dependence upon sense objects. Our minds are bound because of the conception of ego; to loosen these bonds we have to lose our ego. This might seem strange to you, that you should lose your ego. It's certainly not something we talk about in the West. On the contrary, here we are taught to build our egos; if you don't have a strong ego, you're lost, you're not human, you're weak. This seems to be society's view. However, from the point of view of Buddhist psychology, the conception of ego is our biggest problem, the king of problems; other emotions are like ministers, ego is king. When you reach beyond ego, the cabinet of other delusions disappears, the agitated, bound mind vanishes, and you attain an everlasting blissful state of mind. That's what we call nirvana, inner freedom. Your mind is no longer conditioned, tied to something else, like it is at the moment. Presently, because our mind is dependent upon other phenomena, when those other phenomena move, they take our mind with them. We have no control; our mind is led like an animal with a rope through its nose. We are not free; we have no independence. Of course, we think we're free, we think we're independent, but we're not; we're not free inside. Every time the uncontrolled mind arises, we suffer. Therefore, liberation means freedom from dependence upon other conditions and the experience of stable, everlasting bliss, instead of the up and down of our normal lives. That's nirvana. Of course, this is just a brief explanation; we could talk about it for hours, but not now. However, if you understand the nature of inner freedom, you realize that transient sense pleasures are nowhere near enough, that they're not the most important thing. You realize that as a human being you have the ability and the methods to reach a permanent state of everlasting, unconditional joy. That gives you a new perspective on life.

Q: Why do you think that the methods of Buddhist psychology offer an individual a better chance of success in achieving everlasting happiness whereas other methods may have great difficulty in doing this and sometimes never do?

Lama: I'm not saying that because Buddhist methods work we don't need any others. People are different; individual problems require individual solutions. One method won't work for everybody. In the West, you can't say that Christianity offers a solution to all human problems, therefore we don't need psychology or Hinduism or any other philosophy. That's wrong. We need a variety of methods because different people have different personalities and different emotional problems. But the real question we have to ask of any method is can it really put a complete stop to human problems for ever? Actually, Lord Buddha himself taught an amazing variety of psychological remedies to a vast range of problems. Some people think that Buddhism is a rather small subject. In fact, Lord Buddha offered billions of solutions to the countless problems people face. It's almost as if a personalized solution has been given to each individual. Buddhism never says there's just one solution to every problem, that "This is the only way." Lord Buddha gave an incredible variety of solutions to cover every imaginable human problem. Nor is any particular problem necessarily solved all at once. Some problems have to be overcome gradually, by degrees. Buddhist methods also take this into account. That's why we need many approaches.

Q: Sometimes we see patients who are so grossly disturbed that they need large doses of various drugs or just a lot of time before you can even communicate with them. How do you approach someone with whom you can't even communicate intellectually?

Lama: First we try slowly, slowly to become friends in order to earn their trust. Then, when they improve, we start to communicate. Of course, it doesn't always work. The environment is also important—a quiet house in the country; a peaceful place, appropriate pictures, therapeutic colors, that kind of thing. It's difficult.

Q: Some Western psychologists believe that aggression is an important and necessary part of human nature, that anger is a kind of positive driving force, even though it sometimes gets people into trouble. What is your view of anger and aggression?

Lama: I encourage people not to express their anger, not to let it out. Instead, I have people try to understand why they get angry, what causes it and how it arises. When you realize these things, instead of manifesting externally, your anger digests itself. In the West, some people believe that you get rid of anger by expressing it, that you finish it by letting it out. Actually, in this case what happens is that you leave an imprint in your mind to get angry again. The effect is just the opposite of what they believe. It looks like your anger escaped but in fact you're just collecting more anger in your mind. The imprints that anger leaves on your consciousness simply reinforce your tendency to respond to situations with more anger. But not allowing it to come out doesn't mean you are suppressing it, bottling it up. That's also dangerous. You have to learn to investigate the deeper nature of anger, aggression, anxiety or whatever it is that troubles you. When you look into the deeper nature of negative energy you'll see that it's really quite insubstantial, that it's only mind. As your mental expression changes, the negative energy disappears, digested by the wisdom that understands the nature of hatred, anger, aggression and so forth.

Q: Where did the very first moment of anger come from? The anger that left imprint after imprint after imprint?

Lama: Anger comes from attachment to sense pleasure. Check up. This is wonderful psychology, but it can be difficult to understand. When someone touches something to which you are very attached, you freak out. Attachment is the source of anger.

Dr. Gold: Well, Lama, thank you very much for coming and visiting with us. It's been very, very interesting.

Lama: Thank you so much, I'm very happy to have met you all.

Prince Henry's Hospital
Melbourne, Australia
25 March 1975

Everything Comes From the Mind

Buddhism can be understood on many different levels. People who actualize the Buddhist path do so gradually. Just as you pass slowly through school and university, graduating from one year to the next, so do Buddhist practitioners proceed step by step along the path to enlightenment. In Buddhism, however, we're talking about different levels of mind; here, higher and lower refer to spiritual progress.

In the West, there's a tendency to consider Buddhism as a religion in the Western sense of the term. This is a misconception. Buddhism is completely open; we can talk about anything. Buddhism has its doctrine and philosophy, but it also encourages scientific experimentation, both inner and outer. Don't think of Buddhism as some kind of narrow, closed-minded belief system. It isn't. Buddhist doctrine is not a historical fabrication derived through imagination and mental speculation, but an accurate psychological explanation of the actual nature of the mind.

When you look at the outside world you have a very strong impression of its substantiality. You probably don't realize that the strong impression is merely your own mind's interpretation of what it sees. You think that the strong, solid reality really exists outside, and perhaps, when you look within, you feel empty. This is also a misconception: the strong impression that the world appears to truly exist outside of you is actually projected by your own mind. Everything you experience—feelings, sensations, shapes and colors—comes from your mind.

Whether you get up one morning with a foggy mind and the world around you appears to be dark and foggy, or you awaken with a clear mind and your world seems beautiful and light, understand that these different impressions are coming from your own mind rather than from changes in the external environment. Instead of misinterpreting whatever you experience in life through wrong conceptions, realize that it's not outer reality, but only mind.

For example, when everybody in this auditorium looks at a single object—me, Lama Yeshe—each of you has a distinctly different experience, even though simultaneously you are all looking at the one thing. These different experiences don't come from me; they come from your own minds. Perhaps you're thinking, "Oh, how can he say that? We all see the same face, the same body, the same clothes," but that's just a superficial interpretation. Check deeper. You'll see that the way you perceive me, the way you feel, is individual, and that at that level, you're all different. These various perceptions do not come from me but from your own minds. That's the point I'm making.

Then the thought might arise, "Oh, he's just a lama; all he knows about is mind. He doesn't know about powerful scientific advances like satellites and other sophisticated technology. There's no way you can say that those things come from mind." But you check up. When I say "satellite," you have a mental image of the object that you've been told is a satellite. When the first satellite was made, its inventor said, "I've made this thing that orbits the earth; it's called a 'satellite.'" Then when everybody else saw it, they thought, "Ah, that's a satellite." But "satellite" is just a name, isn't it?

Before the inventor of the satellite actually made it, he speculated and visualized it in his mind. On the basis of this image, he acted to materialize his creation. Then he told everyone, "This is a satellite." So everyone thought, "Wow, a satellite; how beautiful, how wonderful." That shows how ridiculous we are. People give things names and we grasp at the name, believing it to be the real thing. It's the same thing no matter what colors and forms we grasp at. You check up.

If you can understand what I'm explaining here, you'll see that indeed, satellites and so forth do come from the mind, and that without mind, there is not a single manifest material existence in the entire sense world. What exists without mind? Look at all the stuff you find in supermarkets: so many names, so many foods, so many different things. First people made it all up—this name, that name, this, this, this—so then, this, that, this, this and this all appear to you. If all these thousands of supermarket items as well as jets, rockets and satellites are manifestations of mind, what then does not come from mind?

If you check into how your mind expresses itself, your various views and feelings, your imagination, you will realize that all your emotions, the way you live your life, the way you relate to others, all come from your own mind. If you don't understand how your mind works, you're going to continue having negative experiences like anger and depression. Why do I call a depressed mind negative? Because a depressed mind doesn't understand how it works. A mind without understanding is negative. A negative mind brings you down because all its reactions are polluted. A mind with understanding functions clearly. A clear mind is a positive mind.

Any emotional problem you experience arises because of the way your mind functions; your basic problem lies in the way you misidentify yourself. Do you normally hold yourself in low esteem, see yourself as a poor quality human being, while what you really want is for your life to be of the highest quality, to be perfect? You don't want to be a poor quality human being, do you? To correct your view and become a better person, you don't need to squeeze yourself or to jump from your own culture into another. All you need to do is to understand your true nature, the way you already are. That's all. It's so simple.

What I'm talking about here is not Tibetan culture, some Eastern trip. I'm talking about your trip. Actually, it doesn't matter whose trip I'm talking about; we're all basically the same. How are we different? We all have mind; we all perceive things through our senses; we are all equal in wanting to enjoy the sense world; and equally we all grasp at the sense world, knowing neither the reality of our inner world nor that of the outer one. There's no difference, whether we have long hair or short, whether we're black, white or red, no matter what clothes we wear. We're all the same. Why?

Because the human mind is like an ocean and we're very similar to each other in the way we've evolved on this earth.

Superficial observation of the sense world might lead you to believe that people's problems are different, but if you check more deeply, you will see that fundamentally, they are the same. What makes people's problems appear to be unique is their different interpretation of their experiences.

This way of checking reality is not necessarily a spiritual exercise. You neither have to believe nor deny that you have a mind—all you have to do is observe how it functions and how you act, and not obsess too much about the world around you.

Lord Buddha never put much emphasis on belief. Instead, he exhorted us to investigate and try to understand the reality of our own being. He never stressed that we had to know what he was, what a buddha is. All he wanted was for us to understand our own nature. Isn't that so simple? We don't have to believe in anything. Simply by making the right effort, we understand things through our own experience, and gradually develop all realizations.

But perhaps you have a question: what about mountains, trees and oceans? How can they come from the mind? I'm going to ask you: what is the nature of a mountain? What is the nature of an ocean? Do things necessarily exist as you see them? When you look at mountains and oceans, they appear to your superficial view as mountains and oceans. But their nature is actually something else. If a hundred people look at a mountain at the same time, they all see different aspects, different colors, different features. Then whose view of the mountain is correct? If you can answer that, you can reply to your own question.

In conclusion, I'm saying that your everyday, superficial view of the sense world does not reflect its true reality. The way you interpret Melbourne, your imagination of how Melbourne exists, has nothing whatsoever to do with the reality of Melbourne—even though you might have been born in Melbourne and have spent your entire up and down life in Melbourne. Check up.

In saying all this, I'm not making a definitive statement but rather offering you a suggestion of how to look at things afresh. I'm not trying to push my own ideas onto you. All I'm doing is recommending that you set aside your usual sluggish mind, which simply takes what it sees at face value, and check with a different mind, a fresh mind.

Most of the decisions that your mind has been making from the time you were born—"This is right; this is wrong; this is not reality"—have been misconceptions. A mind possessed by misconceptions is an uncertain mind, never sure of anything. A small change in the external conditions and it freaks out; even small things make it crazy. If you could only see the whole picture, you'd see how silly this is. But we don't see totality; totality is too big for us.

The wise mind—knowledge-wisdom, or universal consciousness—is never fazed by small things. Seeing totality, it never pays attention to minutiae. Some energy coming from here clashing with some other energy from there never upsets the wise because they expect things like that to happen; it's in their nature. If you have the misconception that your life will be perfect, you will always be shocked by its up and down nature. If you expect your life to be up and down, your mind will be much more peaceful. What in the external world is perfect? Nothing. So since the energy of your mind and body are inextricably bound up with the external world, how can you expect your life to go perfectly? You can't.

Thank you so much. I hope you've understood what I've been saying and that I have not created more wrong conceptions. We have to finish now. Thank you.

Latrobe University
Melbourne, Australia
27 March 1975

MAKE YOUR MIND AN OCEAN

Look into your mind. If you fervently believe that all your enjoyment comes from material objects and dedicate your entire life to their pursuit, you're under the control of a serious misconception. This attitude is not simply an intellectual thing. When you first hear this, you might think, "Oh, I don't have that kind of mind; I don't have complete faith that external objects will bring me happiness." But check more deeply in the mirror of your mind. You will find that beyond the intellect, such an attitude is indeed there and that your everyday actions show that deep within, you really do believe this misconception. Take a moment now to check within yourself to see whether or not you really are under the influence of such an inferior mind.

A mind that has such strong faith in the material world is narrow, limited; it has no space. Its nature is sick, unhealthy, or, in Buddhist terminology, dualistic.

In many countries people are afraid of those who act out of the ordinary, such as those who use drugs. They make laws against the use of drugs and set up elaborate customs controls to catch people smuggling them into the country. Examine this more closely. Drug taking doesn't come from the drug itself but from the person's mind. It would be more sensible to be afraid of the psychological attitude—the polluted mind—that makes people take drugs or engage in other self-destructive behavior, but instead, we make a lot of fuss about the drugs themselves, completely ignoring the role of the mind. This, too, is a serious misconception, much worse than the drugs a few people take.

Misconceptions are much more dangerous than just a few drugs. Drugs themselves don't spread too far, but misconceptions can spread everywhere and cause difficulty and unrest throughout an entire country. All this comes from the mind. The problem is that we don't understand the psychological nature of the mind. We pay attention to only the physical substances that people take; we're totally unaware of the stupid ideas and polluted misconceptions that are crossing borders all the time.

All mental problems come from the mind. We have to treat the mind rather than tell people, "Oh, you're unhappy because you're feeling weak. What you need is a powerful new car..." or some other kind of material possession. Telling people to go buy something to be happy is not wise advice. The person's basic problem is mental dissatisfaction, not a lack of material possessions. When it comes to the approach to mental problems and how to treat patients, there's a big difference between Lord Buddha's psychology and that which is practiced in the West.

When the patient returns and says, "Well, I bought the car you recommended but I'm still unhappy," perhaps the doctor will say, "You should have bought a more expensive one" or "You should have chosen a better color." Even if he goes away and does that, he's still going to come back unhappy. No matter how many superficial changes are made to a person's environment, his problems won't stop. Buddhist psychology recommends that, instead of constantly substituting one agitated condition for another—thereby simply changing one problem into another and then another and then another without end—give up cars completely for a while and see what happens. Sublimating one problem into another solves nothing; it's merely change. Though change may often be enough to fool people into thinking they're getting better, they're not. Basically they're still experiencing the same thing. Of course, I don't mean all this literally. I'm simply trying to illustrate how people try to solve mental problems through physical means.

Recognize the nature of your mind. As human beings, we always seek satisfaction. By knowing the nature of the mind, we can satisfy ourselves internally; perhaps even eternally. But you must realize the nature of your own mind. We see the sense world so clearly, but we're

completely blind to our internal world, where the constant functioning of misconceptions keeps us under the control of unhappiness
and dissatisfaction. This is what we must discover.

It is crucial, therefore, to make sure that you are not laboring
under the misconception that only external objects can give you satisfaction or make your life worthwhile. As I said before, this belief
is not simply intellectual—the long root of this delusion reaches
deep into your mind. Many of your strongest desires are buried far
below your intellect; that which lies beneath the intellect is usually
much stronger than the intellect itself.

Some people might think, "My basic psychology is sound. I
don't have faith in materials; I'm a student of religion." Simply having learned some religious philosophy or doctrine doesn't make you
a spiritual person. Many university professors can give clear intellectual explanations of Buddhism, Hinduism and Christianity, but
that alone doesn't make them spiritual people. They're more like
tourist guides for the spiritually curious. If you can't put your words
into experience, your learning helps neither yourselves nor others.
There's a big difference between being able to explain religion intellectually and transforming that knowledge into spiritual experience.

You have to put what you've learned into your own experience
and understand the results that various actions bring. A cup of tea
is probably of more use than learned scholarship of a philosophy
that cannot support your mind because you don't have the key—at
least it quenches your thirst. Studying a philosophy that doesn't
function is a waste of time and energy.

I hope that you understand what the word "spiritual" really
means. It means to search for, to investigate, the true nature of the
mind. There's nothing spiritual outside. My rosary isn't spiritual; my
robes aren't spiritual. Spiritual means the mind, and spiritual people
are those who seek its nature. Through this, they come to understand
the effects of their behavior, the actions of their body, speech and
mind. If you don't understand the karmic results of what you think
and do, there's no way for you to become a spiritual person. Just knowing some religious philosophy isn't enough to make you spiritual.

To enter the spiritual path, you must begin to understand your own mental attitude and how your mind perceives things. If you're all caught up in attachment to tiny atoms, your limited, craving mind will make it impossible for you to enjoy life's pleasures. External energy is so incredibly limited that if you allow yourself to be bound by it, your mind itself will become just as limited. When your mind is narrow, small things agitate you very easily. Make your mind an ocean.

We hear religious people talk a lot about morality. What is morality? Morality is the wisdom that understands the nature of the mind. The mind that understands its own nature automatically becomes moral, or positive; and the actions motivated by such a mind also become positive. That's what we call morality. The basic nature of the narrow mind is ignorance; therefore the narrow mind is negative.

If you know the psychological nature of your own mind, depression is spontaneously dispelled; instead of being enemies and strangers, all living beings become your friends. The narrow mind rejects; wisdom accepts. Check your own mind to see whether or not this is true. Even if you were to get every possible sense pleasure that the universe could offer, you would still not be satisfied. That shows that satisfaction comes from within, not from anything external.

Sometimes we marvel at the modern world: "What fantastic advances scientific technology has made; how wonderful! We never had these things before." But step back and take another look. Many of the things we thought fantastic not so long ago are now rising up against us. Things we developed to help our lives are now hurting us. Don't just look at your immediate surroundings, but check as widely as possible; you'll see the truth of what I'm saying. When we first create material things we think, "Oh, this is useful." But gradually this external energy turns inward and destroys itself. Such is the nature of the four elements: earth, water, fire and air. This is what Buddhist science teaches us.

Your body is no exception to this rule. As long as your elements are cooperating with each other, your body grows beautifully. But after a while the elements turn against themselves and finish up destroying your life. Why does this happen? Because of the limited nature of material phenomena: when their power is exhausted, they collapse, like the old and crumbling buildings we see around us. When our bodies become sick and decrepit it's a sign that our internal energies are in conflict, out of balance. This is the nature of the material world; it has nothing to do with faith. As long as we keep being born into the meat, blood and bone of the human body, we're going to experience bad conditions, whether we believe it or not. This is the natural evolution of the worldly body.

The human mind, however, is completely different. The human mind has the potential for infinite development. If you can discover, even in a small way, that true satisfaction comes from your mind, you will realize that you can extend this experience without limit and that it is possible to discover everlasting satisfaction.

It's actually very simple. You can check for yourself right now. Where do you experience the feeling of satisfaction? In your nose? Your eye? Your head? Your lung? Your heart? Your stomach? Where is that feeling of satisfaction? In your leg? Your hand? Your brain? No! It's in your mind. If you say it's in your brain, why can't you say it's in your nose or your leg? Why do you differentiate? If your leg hurts, you feel it down there, not inside your head. Anyway, whatever pain, pleasure or other feeling you experience, it's all an expression of mind.

When you say, "I had a good day today," it shows that you're holding in your mind the memory of a bad day. Without the mind creating labels, there's neither good experience nor bad. When you say that tonight's dinner was good, it means that you're holding the experience of a bad dinner in mind. Without the experience of a bad dinner it's impossible for you to call tonight's good.

Similarly, "I'm a good husband," "I'm a bad wife," are also merely expressions of mind. Someone who says, "I am bad" is not necessarily bad; someone who says, "I am good" is not necessarily good. Perhaps the man who says, "I'm such a good husband" does so because his mind is full of the disturbing negative mind of pride. His narrow mind, stuck in the deluded, concrete belief that he's good, actually causes much difficulty for his wife. How, then, is he a good husband? Even if he does provide food and clothing for his wife, how can he be a good husband, when day after day she has to live with his arrogance?

If you can understand the psychological aspects of human problems, you can really generate true loving-kindness towards others. Just talking about loving-kindness doesn't help you develop it. Some people may have read about loving-kindness hundreds of times but their minds are the very opposite. It's not just philosophy, not just words; it's knowing how the mind functions. Only then can you develop loving-kindness; only then can you become a spiritual person. Otherwise, though you might be convinced you're a spiritual person, it's just intellectual, like the arrogant man who believes he's a good husband. It's a fiction; your mind just makes it up.

It is so worthwhile that you devote your precious human life to controlling your mad elephant mind and giving direction to your powerful mental energy. If you don't harness your mental energy, confusion will continue to rage through your mind and your life will be completely wasted. Be as wise with your own mind as you possibly can. That makes your life worthwhile.

I don't have much else to tell you, but if you have any questions, please ask.

Q: I understand what you said about knowing the nature of your own mind bringing you happiness, but you used the term "everlasting," which implies that if you understand your mind completely, you can transcend death of the physical body. Is this correct?
Lama: Yes, that's right. But that's not all. If you know how, when negative physical energy arises, you can convert it into wisdom. In this way your negative energy digests itself and doesn't end up blocking your psychic nervous system. That's possible.

Q: Is the mind body, or is the body mind?
Lama: What do you mean?

Q: Because I perceive the body.

Lama: Because you perceive it? Do you perceive this rosary [holding it up]?

Q: Yes.

Lama: Does that make it mind? Because you perceive it?

Q: That's what I'm asking you.

Lama: Well, that's a good question. Your body and mind are very strongly connected; when something affects your body it also affects your mind. But that doesn't mean that the relative nature of your physical body, its meat and bone, is mind. You can't say that.

Q: What are the aims of Buddhism: enlightenment, brotherhood, universal love, super consciousness, realization of the truth, the attainment of nirvana?

Lama: All of the above: super consciousness, the fully awakened state of mind, universal love, and an absence of partiality or bias based on the realization that all living beings throughout the universe are equal in wanting to be happy and to avoid feeling unhappy. At the moment, our dualistic, wrong-conception minds discriminate: "This is my close friend, I want to keep her for myself and not share her with others." One of Buddhism's aims is to attain the opposite of this, universal love. Of course, the ultimate goal is enlightenment. In short, the aim of Lord Buddha's teachings on the nature of the mind is for us to gain all those realizations you mentioned.

Q: But which is considered to be the highest or most important aim?

Lama: The highest aims are enlightenment and the development of universal love. The narrow mind finds it difficult to experience such realizations.

Q: In Tibetan paintings, how do colors correspond with states of meditation or different psychological states?

Lama: Different kinds of mind perceive different colors. We say that when we are angry we see red. That's a good example. Other states of mind visualize their own respective colors. In some cases, where people are emotionally disturbed and unable to function in their daily lives, surrounding them with certain colors can help settle them down. If you think about this you will discover that color really comes from the mind. When you get angry and see red, is that color internal or external? Think about it.

Q: What are the practical, daily life implications of your saying that in order to have the idea that something is good you must also have in your mind the idea of bad?

Lama: I was saying that when you interpret things as good or bad it's your own mind's interpretation. What's bad for you is not necessarily bad for me.

Q: But my bad is still my bad.

Lama: Your bad is bad for you because your mind calls it bad.

Q: Can I go beyond that?

Lama: Yes, you can go beyond that. You have to ask and answer the question, "Why do I call this bad?" You have to question both the object and the subject, both the external and the internal situations. In that way you can realize that the reality is somewhere in between, that in the space between the two there's a unified mind. That's wisdom.

Q: How old were you when you entered the monastery?

Lama: I was six.

Q: What is nirvana?

Lama: When you transcend the wrong-conception, agitated mind and attain fully integrated, everlastingly satisfied wisdom, you have reached nirvana.

Q: Every religion says that it is the one way to enlightenment. Does Buddhism recognize all religions as coming from the same source?

Lama: There are two ways of answering that question, the absolute and the relative. Religions that emphasize the attainment of enlightenment are probably talking about the same thing, but where they differ is in their approach, in their methods. I think this is helpful. But it's also true that some religions may be based on misconceptions. Nevertheless, I don't repudiate them. For example, a couple of thousand years ago there were some ancient Hindu traditions that believed the sun and moon to be gods; some of them still exist. From my point of view, those conceptions are wrong, but I still say that they're good. Why? Because even though philosophically they're incorrect, they still teach the basic morality of being a good human being and not harming others. That gives their followers the possibility of reaching the point where they discover for themselves, "Oh, I used to believe that the sun was a god but now I see I was wrong." Therefore, there's good in every religion and we should not judge, "This is totally right; that is totally wrong."

Q: As far as you know, what is life like for people in Tibet these days? Are they free to pursue their Buddhist religion as before?

Lama: They are not free and are completely prohibited from any religious practice. The Chinese authorities are totally against anything to do with religion. Monasteries have been destroyed and sacred scriptures burned.

Q: But even though their books have been burned, do the older people still keep the Dharma in their hearts and minds, or have they forgotten everything?

Lama: It's impossible to forget, to separate their minds from such powerful wisdom. So the Dharma remains in their hearts.

Q: All religions, for example, Hinduism, teach their adherents to avoid evil actions and to practice good ones and that good karmic results will ensue. How, according to Buddhism, does this accumulation of positive karma help one attain enlightenment?

Lama: Mental development does not happen through radical change. Defilements are eliminated, or purified, slowly, slowly. There's a gradual evolution. It takes time. Some people, for instance, cannot accept what Buddhism teaches about universal love, that you should want others to have the happiness that you want for yourself. They feel, "It's impossible for me to love all others as I love myself." It takes time for them to realize universal love or enlightenment because their minds are preoccupied by misconceptions and there's no space for wisdom. But slowly, slowly, through practicing their religion, people can be led to perfect wisdom. That's why I say that a variety of religions is necessary for the human race. Physical change is easy, but mental development takes time. For example, a doctor might tell a sick person, "Your temperature is very high, so please avoid meat and eat only dry biscuits for a few days." Then, as the person starts to recover, the doctor slowly reintroduces heavy food into his diet. In that way the doctor gradually leads the person back to perfect health.

Q: When Tibetan monks and nuns die, do their bodies disappear, do they take their bodies with them?

Lama: Yes, they carry them to their next lives in their *jola* [monk's shoulder bag]…I'm joking! No, that's impossible. Still, there are certain practitioners whose bodies are digested into wisdom and actually disappear. That's possible. But they don't take their bodies with them physically.

Q: Since our minds can deceive us, and without a teacher we can't discover the truth, are Buddhist monasteries designed so that each monk pulls his colleagues up to the next step of knowledge, in a sort of chain? Is that what you're doing now, and do you teach in order to learn?

Lama: Yes, monasteries are something like that, and it's also true that I learn as I teach. But why we need teachers is because book knowledge is just dry information and if left as such can be as relevant as the wind whistling through the trees. We need a key to put it into experience, to unify that knowledge with our minds. Then knowledge becomes wisdom and the perfect solution to problems. For example, the Bible is an excellent book that contains all kinds of great methods, but if you don't have the key, the knowledge that's in the Bible doesn't enter your heart. Just because a book is excellent doesn't necessarily mean that by reading it you'll gain the knowledge it contains. The only way that can happen is for your mind to first develop wisdom.

Q: You said that getting enlightened is a gradual process, but surely you can't be both enlightened and unenlightened at the same time. Wouldn't that mean, therefore, that enlightenment is sudden?
Lama: Of course, you're right. You can't be enlightened and ignorant together. Approaching enlightenment is a gradual process, but once you attain it, there's no going back; when you reach the fully awakened state of mind, the moment you experience that, you remain enlightened forever. It's not like some hallucinatory drug experience—when you're high you're having a good time, and when the effect of the drug wears off you're back down to your usual depressed self.

Q: And we can experience that in this life, permanent enlightenment, while we're still alive, before we die?
Lama: Yes, that's possible. In this life...if you have enough wisdom.

Q: Oh...if you have enough wisdom?
Lama: Yes...that's the catch: if you have enough wisdom.

Q: Why do we need a teacher?
Lama: Why do you need an English teacher? For communication. It's the same thing with enlightenment. Enlightenment is also communication. Even for mundane activities like shopping we need to learn the language so that we can communicate with the shopkeepers. If we need teachers for that, of course we need someone to guide

us along a path that deals with so many unknowns like past and future lives and deep levels of consciousness. These are entirely new experiences; you don't know where you're going or what's happening. You need someone to make sure you're on the right track and not hallucinating.

Q: Who taught the first teacher?
Lama: Wisdom. The first teacher was wisdom.

Q: Well, if the first teacher didn't have a human teacher, why do any of us need one?
Lama: Because there's no beginning, and there's no end. Wisdom is universal wisdom, wisdom is universal consciousness.

Q: Does generating universal love bring you to enlightenment or do you first have to reach enlightenment and then generate universal love?
Lama: First you generate universal love. Then your mind attains the realization of equilibrium, where you emphasize neither this nor that. Your mind attains a state of balance. In Buddhist terminology, you reach beyond the dualistic mind.

Q: Is it true that the mind can only take you so far on the spiritual path and that at some point, in order to go further, you have to give up your mind?
Lama: How can you give up your mind? I'm joking. No, it's impossible for you to abandon your mind. While you're a human, living what we call an ordinary life, you have mind; when you reach enlightenment, you still have mind. Your mind is always with you. You can't get rid of it simply by saying, "I don't want to have a mind." Karmically, your mind and body are stuck together. It's impossible to relinquish your mind intellectually. If your mind were a material phenomenon, perhaps you could, but it's not.

Q: Do lamas ever become physically ill, and if so, what method do you use to overcome the illness? Do you use healing power?

Lama: Yes, sometimes we use healing power; sometimes we use the power of mantra; sometimes we meditate. At certain other times we do *puja.* Do you know what that is? Some people think it's just ritual chanting and bell ringing, but it's much more than that. Puja is a Sanskrit word whose literal meaning is "offering"; but its interpretive meaning is wisdom, an awakened state of mind. So, if your wisdom is ringing, "ting, ting, ting," that's good, but if your wisdom isn't ringing and the only ting, ting, ting you hear is the external one, then that's no puja.

Q: What you're saying is not that far removed from Western materialist philosophy. Our problems are not so much with objects as with our attitude towards them.

Lama: When you say attitude, are you referring to the mental tendency to grasp or not to grasp at material objects?

Q: Well, external objects do exist, but they exist outside of ourselves, and our consciousness perceives them on the same plane. I believe that when we die, the objects remain, but not for us, not for the individual.

Lama: I agree with you. When we die, the external objects are still there, but our interpretation of them, our projection, disappears. Yes, that's right.

Q: So how is that so radically opposed to materialistic philosophy? Why do you say that the external world is illusory when after our consciousness departs, the material world remains?

Lama: I say that the material world is illusory because the objects you perceive exist only in the view of your own mind. Look at this table: the problem is that you think that when you disappear, your view of this table still exists, that this table continues to exist just the way you saw it. That's not true. Your view of the table disappears, but another view of the table continues to exist.

Q: How can we recognize the right teacher?

Lama: You can recognize your teacher through using your own wisdom and not just following someone blindly. Investigate potential teachers as much as you possibly can. "Is this the right teacher for me or not?" Check deeply before you follow any teacher's advice. In Tibetan we have an admonition not to take a teacher like a dog seizes a piece of meat. If you give a hungry dog a piece of meat he'll just gobble it up without hesitation. It is crucial that you examine possible spiritual leaders, teachers, gurus or whatever you call them very, very carefully before accepting their guidance. Remember what I said before about misconceptions and polluted doctrines being more dangerous than drugs? If you follow the misconceptions of a false spiritual guide it can have a disastrous effect on you and cause you to waste not only this life but many others as well. Instead of helping you, it can bring you great harm. Please, be very wise in choosing your spiritual teacher.

Q: Since you are a Buddhist monk from Tibet, I'm wondering if you've heard of Lobsang Rampa, who has written many detailed books about Tibet despite having never been there himself? He's dead now, but he said that the spirit of a Tibetan lama entered him and that's how he could write what he did. Is that possible, and if not, how could he have written those books?

Lama: I don't think that this kind of possession is possible. Also, you should check what he wrote more carefully; there are many mistakes in his books. For example, when he talks about lamas opening the wisdom eye he says it's done surgically. That's not right. The wisdom eye is a metaphor for spiritual insight and it's opened by lamas who have the key of wisdom. Also, those who have realizations don't talk about them, and those who talk about their realizations don't have them.

Q: Lama, what do you mean by dualistic mind, and what do you mean by "checking up"?

Lama: From the time you were born up to the present, two things have always complicated your mind; there are always two things, never just one. That's what we mean by the dualistic mind. Whenever you see one thing, your mind automatically, instinctively, compares it to something else: "What about that?" Those two things upset your equilibrium. That's the dualistic mind at work. Now, your other question. When I say, "check up," I mean that you should investigate your own mind to see if it's healthy or not. Every morning, check your mental state to make sure that during the day you don't freak out. That's all I mean by "check up."

Q: If everything is karmically determined, how do we know if our motivation is correct, or do we have a chance of unconditioned choice?

Lama: Pure motivation is not determined by karma. Pure motivation comes from understanding-knowledge-wisdom. If there's no understanding in your mind it's difficult for your motivation to be pure. For example, if I don't understand my own selfish nature, I can't help others. As long as I don't recognize my selfish behavior, I always blame others for my problems. When I know my own mind, my motivation becomes pure and I can sincerely dedicate the actions of my body, speech and mind to the welfare of others.

Thank you, that was a wonderful question, and I think that pure motivation is a good place to stop. Thank you so much. If we have pure motivation, we sleep well, dream well and enjoy well, so thank you very much.

Assembly Hall
Melbourne, Australia
27 March 1975

THE LAMA YESHE WISDOM ARCHIVE

The LAMA YESHE WISDOM ARCHIVE (LYWA) is the collected works of Lama Thubten Yeshe and Lama Thubten Zopa Rinpoche. The ARCHIVE was founded in 1996 by Lama Zopa Rinpoche, its spiritual director, to make available in various ways the teachings it contains. Distribution of free booklets of edited teachings is one of the ways.

Lama Yeshe and Lama Zopa Rinpoche began teaching at Kopan Monastery, Nepal, in 1970. Since then, their teachings have been recorded and transcribed. At present the LYWA contains more than 7,000 cassette tapes, all of which have now been digitized, and approximately 50,000 pages of transcribed teachings on computer disk. Many tapes, mostly teachings by Lama Zopa Rinpoche, remain to be transcribed. As Rinpoche continues to teach, the number of tapes in the ARCHIVE increases accordingly. Most of the transcripts have been neither checked nor edited.

Here at the LYWA we are making every effort to organize the transcription of that which has not yet been transcribed, to edit that which has not yet been edited, and generally to do the many other tasks detailed opposite. In all this, we need your help. Please contact us for more information:

LAMA YESHE WISDOM ARCHIVE
PO Box 356
Weston MA 02493, USA
Telephone (781) 899-9587; Fax (413) 845-9239
info@LamaYeshe.com
www.LamaYeshe.com

THE ARCHIVE TRUST

The work of the LAMA YESHE WISDOM ARCHIVE falls into two categories: archiving and dissemination.

Archiving requires managing the audiotapes of teachings by Lama Yeshe and Lama Zopa Rinpoche that have already been collected, collecting recordings of teachings given but not yet sent to the ARCHIVE, and collecting recordings of Lama Zopa's on-going teachings, talks, advice and so forth as he travels the world for the benefit of all. Tapes and disks are then catalogued and stored safely while being kept accessible for further work.

We organize the transcription of tapes, add the transcripts to the already existent database of teachings, manage this database, have transcripts checked, and make transcripts available to editors or others doing research on or practicing these teachings.

Other archiving activities include working with videotapes and photographs of the Lamas and digitizing ARCHIVE materials.

Dissemination involves making the Lamas' teachings available directly or indirectly through various avenues such as booklets for free distribution, regular books for the trade, lightly edited transcripts, floppy disks, audio- and videotapes and CDs, and articles in *Mandala* and other magazines, and on our Web site. Irrespective of the method we choose, the teachings require a significant amount of work to prepare them for distribution.

This is just a summary of what we do. The ARCHIVE was established with virtually no seed funding and has developed solely through the kindness of many people, some of whom we have mentioned at the front of this book and most of the others on our Web site. We sincerely thank them all.

Our further development similarly depends upon the generosity of those who see the benefit and necessity of this work, and we would be extremely grateful for your help.

The ARCHIVE TRUST has been established to fund the above activities and we hereby appeal to you for your kind support. If you would like to make a contribution to help us with any of the above tasks or to sponsor booklets for free distribution, please contact us at our Weston address.

The LAMA YESHE WISDOM ARCHIVE is a 501(c)(3) tax-deductible, non-profit corporation (ID number 04-3374479) dedicated to the welfare of all sentient beings and totally dependent upon your donations for its continued existence.

Thank you so much for your support. You may contribute by mailing a check, bank draft or money order to our Weston address; by making a donation on our secure Web site; by mailing or faxing us your credit card number or by phoning it in; or by transferring funds directly to our bank—ask us for details.

THE FOUNDATION FOR THE PRESERVATION OF THE MAHAYANA TRADITION

The Foundation for the Preservation of the Mahayana Tradition (FPMT) is an international organization of Buddhist meditation study and retreat centers, both urban and rural, monasteries, publishing houses, healing centers and other related activities founded in 1975 by Lama Thubten Yeshe and Lama Thubten Zopa Rinpoche. At present, there are more than 150 FPMT activities in over thirty countries worldwide.

The FPMT has been established to facilitate the study and practice of Mahayana Buddhism in general and the Tibetan Gelug tradition, founded in the fifteenth century by the great scholar, yogi and saint, Lama Je Tsong Khapa, in particular.

Every three months, the Foundation publishes a magazine, *Mandala,* from its International Office in the United States of America. To subscribe or view back issues, please go to the *Mandala* Web site, www.mandalamagazine.org, or contact:

FPMT
PO Box 888, Taos, NM 87571, USA
Telephone (505) 758-7766; fax (505) 758-7765
fpmtinfo@fpmt.org • www.fpmt.org

Our Web site also offers teachings by His Holiness the Dalai Lama, Lama Yeshe, Lama Zopa Rinpoche and many other highly respected teachers in the tradition, details about the FPMT's educational programs, audio through FPMT radio, a complete listing of FPMT centers all over the world and in your area, and links to FPMT centers on the Web, where you will find details of their programs, and to other interesting Buddhist and Tibetan home pages.

OTHER TEACHINGS OF
LAMA YESHE AND LAMA ZOPA RINPOCHE
CURRENTLY AVAILABLE

BOOKS PUBLISHED BY WISDOM PUBLICATIONS

Wisdom Energy, by Lama Yeshe and Lama Zopa Rinpoche
Introduction to Tantra, by Lama Yeshe
Transforming Problems, by Lama Zopa Rinpoche
The Door to Satisfaction, by Lama Zopa Rinpoche
The Tantric Path of Purification, by Lama Yeshe
The Bliss of Inner Fire, by Lama Yeshe
Ultimate Healing, by Lama Zopa Rinpoche
Becoming the Compassion Buddha, by Lama Yeshe

You may see more information about and order the above titles at the Wisdom Web site, www.wisdompubs.org, or call toll free in the USA on 1-800-272-4050.

TRANSCRIPTS

Several transcripts of teachings by Lama Yeshe and Lama Zopa Rinpoche are also available. See the LAMA YESHE WISDOM ARCHIVE Web site for more details.

VIDEOS OF LAMA YESHE

We are in the process of converting our VHS videos of Lama Yeshe's teachings to CD. See our Web site for more information.

VIDEOS OF LAMA ZOPA RINPOCHE

See the FPMT Web site for more information. You will also find there many recommended practices written or compiled by Rinpoche.

What to do with Dharma teachings

The Buddhadharma is the true source of happiness for all sentient beings. Books like this show you how to put the teachings into practice and integrate them into your life, whereby you get the happiness you seek. Therefore, anything containing Dharma teachings or the names of your teachers is more precious than other material objects and should be treated with respect. To avoid creating the karma of not meeting the Dharma again in future lives, please do not put books (or other holy objects) on the floor or underneath other stuff, step over or sit upon them, or use them for mundane purposes such as propping up wobbly tables. They should be kept in a clean, high place, separate from worldly writings, and wrapped in cloth when being carried around. These are but a few considerations.

Should you need to get rid of Dharma materials, they should not be thrown in the rubbish but burned in a special way. Briefly: do not incinerate such materials with other trash, but alone, and as they burn, recite the mantra OM AH HUM. As the smoke rises, visualize that it pervades all of space, carrying the essence of the Dharma to all sentient beings in the six samsaric realms, purifying their minds, alleviating their suffering, and bringing them all happiness, up to and including enlightenment. Some people might find this practice a bit unusual, but it is given according to tradition. Thank you very much.

Dedication

Through the merit created by preparing, reading, thinking about and sharing this book with others, may all teachers of the Dharma live long and healthy lives, may the Dharma spread throughout the infinite reaches of space, and may all sentient beings quickly attain enlightenment.

In whichever realm, country, area or place this book may be, may there be no war, drought, famine, disease, injury, disharmony or unhappiness, may there be only great prosperity, may every thing needed be easily obtained, and may all be guided by only perfectly qualified Dharma teachers, enjoy the happiness of Dharma, have only love and compassion for all beings, and only benefit and never harm each other.

LAMA THUBTEN YESHE was born in Tibet in 1935. At the age of six, he entered the great Sera Monastic University, Lhasa, where he studied until 1959, when the Chinese invasion of Tibet forced him into exile in India. Lama Yeshe continued to study and meditate in India until 1967, when, with his chief disciple, Lama Thubten Zopa Rinpoche, he went to Nepal. Two years later he established Kopan Monastery, near Kathmandu, in order to teach Buddhism to Westerners. In 1974, the Lamas began making annual teaching tours to the West, and as a result of these travels a worldwide network of Buddhist teaching and meditation centers—the Foundation for the Preservation of the Mahayana Tradition—began to develop. In 1984, after an intense decade of imparting a wide variety of incredible teachings and establishing one FPMT activity after another, at the age of forty-nine, Lama Yeshe passed away. He was reborn as Osel Hita Torres in Spain in 1985, recognized as the incarnation of Lama Yeshe by His Holiness the Dalai Lama in 1986, and, as the monk Lama Tenzin Osel Rinpoche, is studying for his geshe degree at the reconstituted Sera Monastery in South India. Lama's remarkable story is told in Vicki Mackenzie's book, *Reincarnation: The Boy Lama* (Wisdom Publications, 1996).

Some of Lama Yeshe's teachings have also been published by Wisdom. Books include *Wisdom Energy; Introduction to Tantra; The Tantric Path of Purification; The Bliss of Inner Fire;* and *Becoming the Compassion Buddha.* Transcripts in print are *Light of Dharma; Life, Death and After Death;* and *Transference of Consciousness at the Time of Death.* Available through FPMT centers or at www.wisdompubs.org. Other teachings may be found on line at www.LamaYeshe.com.

Lama Yeshe on video: *Introduction to Tantra* and *The Three Principal Aspects of the Path.* Available from the LAMA YESHE WISDOM ARCHIVE.

DR. NICHOLAS RIBUSH, MB, BS, is a graduate of Melbourne University Medical School (1964) who first encountered Buddhism at Kopan Monastery, Nepal, in 1972. Since then he has been a student of Lama Yeshe and Lama Zopa Rinpoche and a full time worker for their international organization, the Foundation for the Preservation of the Mahayana Tradition (FPMT). He was a monk from 1974 to 1986. He established FPMT archiving and publishing activities at Kopan in 1973, and with Lama Yeshe founded Wisdom Publications in 1975. Between 1981 and 1996 he served variously as Wisdom's director, editorial director and director of development. Over the years he has edited and published many teachings by Lama Yeshe and Lama Zopa Rinpoche, and established and/or directed several other FPMT activities, including the International Mahayana Institute, Tushita Mahayana Meditation Centre, the Enlightened Experience Celebration, Mahayana Publications, Kurukulla Center for Tibetan Buddhist Studies and now the LAMA YESHE WISDOM ARCHIVE. He was a member of the FPMT board of directors from its inception in 1983 until 2002.